NEURODEVELOPMENTAL DISEASES:
LABORATORY AND CLINICAL RESEARCH

ADVANCES IN AUTISM SPECTRUM DISORDER RESEARCH

SUMMARIES, 2007-2011

NEURODEVELOPMENTAL DISEASES: LABORATORY AND CLINICAL RESEARCH

Additional books in this series can be found on Nova's website under the Series tab.

Additional E-books in this series can be found on Nova's website under the E-book tab.

NEUROSCIENCE RESEARCH PROGRESS

Additional books in this series can be found on Nova's website under the Series tab.

Additional E-books in this series can be found on Nova's website under the E-book tab.

NEURODEVELOPMENTAL DISEASES: LABORATORY AND CLINICAL RESEARCH

ADVANCES IN AUTISM SPECTRUM DISORDER RESEARCH

SUMMARIES, 2007-2011

RICHARD L. JACKSON
AND
ANTHONY C. LEE
EDITORS

Nova Science Publishers, Inc.
New York

For permission to use material from this book please contact us:
Telephone 631-231-7269; Fax 631-231-8175
Web Site: http://www.novapublishers.com

Library of Congress Cataloging-in-Publication Data

ISBN: 978-1-62257-058-4

Published by Nova Science Publishers, Inc. † New York

CONTENTS

PREFACE

There is an urgent need for increased knowledge about all aspects of autism spectrum disorder (ASD), from identifying risk factors, to understanding underlying biology, to developing new more effective treatments, to bringing evidence based practices into the community. Over the past decade, research addressing these issues has expanded dramatically due to greater availability of resources and wider appreciation of the individual, family, and societal costs of ASD. To comprehend the current state of ASD research and begin to plan next steps, Congress requested an annual update of scientific advances. This book is a summary on the advances in autism spectrum disorder research that has been ongoing from calendar years 2007 through 2011.

Chapter 1- There is an urgent need for increased knowledge about all aspects of autism spectrum disorder (ASD), from identifying risk factors, to understanding underlying biology, to developing new more effective treatments, to bringing evidence based practices into the community. Over the past decade, research addressing these issues has expanded dramatically due to greater availability of resources and wider appreciation of the individual, family, and societal costs of ASD.

To comprehend the current state of ASD research and begin to plan the next steps, Congress requested an annual update of scientific advances. Specifically, the Combating Autism Act (CAA) of 2006 (P.L. 109-416) requires the Interagency Autism Coordinating Committee to develop and annually update a summary of advances in ASD research.

ASD includes a range of developmental disorders than share common features including impaired communication skills and social interactions, and restricted, repetitive, and stereotyped patterns of behavior. Due to its complexity, increasing our understanding of ASD requires new knowledge from various fields of study such as neuroscience, genetics, immunology, biology, psychology, and pharmacology.

Chapter 2- The dramatic increase in the prevalence of autism spectrum disorders (ASD) over the past two decades has spurred research into all aspects of the disorders. Researchers are now doing critical work to understand what causes ASD, how it can be effectively treated, and how to improve the lives of those affected.

ASD includes a range of developmental disorders that share common features including impaired communication skills and social interactions and restricted, repetitive, and stereotyped patterns of behavior. Currently, the Centers for Disease Control and Prevention (CDC) estimates that about 1 in 150 children in the United States has ASD.

In response to the alarming growth in autism diagnoses, Congress passed the Combating Autism Act of 2006 (P.L. 109-416), which established the Interagency Autism Coordinating Committee (IACC) to coordinate all efforts within the U.S. Department of Health and Human Services related to ASD. The Combating Autism Act requires that, in addition to several other key responsibilities, the IACC must prepare an annual summary of advances in autism research.

Chapter 3- Each year the members of the Interagency Autism Coordinating Committee identify recent research findings that made the most impact on the field. For the 2009 Summary of Advances, the IACC selected and summarized 20 studies that gave significant insight into the prevalence of autism spectrum disorder, the biology of the disorder, potential risk factors, and possible interventions. These articles were the top selections from a pool of 63 peer-reviewed articles published in 2009 that were nominated by the committee to reflect the most important work in biomedical and services research for ASD during the year — work that is critical to understanding the disorder and addressing the needs of people with ASD and their families. (Articles appear in alphabetical order by first author. A full reference.

Chapter 4- As part of the Combating Autism Act of 2006, the members of the Interagency Autism Coordinating Committee are required to develop an annual "Summary of Advances" to describe each year's top advances in autism spectrum disorder research.

These advances represent significant progress in the early diagnosis of ASD, understanding the complex biology of the disorder, and identifying potential risk factors.

They may also relate to work identifying effective treatments and services and studies of the national prevalence of ASD and necessary research infrastructure.

The 2010 Summary of Advances provides short, plain language synopses of the top twenty research breakthroughs selected by the committee from a pool of 64 peer-reviewed articles nominated by the members. Articles are grouped according to the questions of the IACC Strategic Plan for ASD Research (available at www.iacc.hhs.gov).

Citations for the articles selected for the Summary of Advances, as wellas a complete listing of those nominated, are included at the end of the document.

Chapter 5- Each year the IACC releases its annual list of scientific advances that represent significant progress in the field. The twenty studies selected have given new insight into the complex causes of autism and potential risk factors, studied clues that could lead to earlier diagnosis, and evaluated promising early intervention strategies. The advances also address the prevalence of ASD both in the U.S. and internationally, as well as the service needs of people with ASD across the lifespan. The 2011 Summary of Advances provides short, plain language synopses of the top research breakthroughs selected by the committee from a pool of peer-reviewed articles nominated by the members. Articles are grouped according to the questions of the IACC Strategic Plan for ASD Research (available at www.iacc.hhs.gov). Citations for the articles selected for the Summary of Advances, as well as a complete listing of those nominated, are included at the end of the document.

In: Advances in Autism Spectrum Disorder ... ISBN: 978-1-62257-058-4
Editors: R. L. Jackson and A. C. Lee

Chapter 1

SUMMARY OF ADVANCES IN AUTISM SPECTRUM DISORDER RESEARCH: CALENDAR YEAR 2007*

Interagency Autism Coordinating Committee

INTRODUCTION

There is an urgent need for increased knowledge about all aspects of autism spectrum disorder (ASD), from identifying risk factors, to understanding underlying biology, to developing new more effective treatments, to bringing evidence based practices into the community. Over the past decade, research addressing these issues has expanded dramatically due to greater availability of resources and wider appreciation of the individual, family, and societal costs of ASD.

To comprehend the current state of ASD research and begin to plan the next steps, Congress requested an annual update of scientific advances. Specifically, the Combating Autism Act (CAA) of 2006 (P.L. 109-416) requires the Interagency Autism Coordinating Committee to develop and annually update a summary of advances in ASD research.

ASD includes a range of developmental disorders than share common features including impaired communication skills and social interactions, and restricted, repetitive, and stereotyped patterns of behavior. Due to its

---

* This is an edited, reformatted and augmented version of an Interagency Autism Coordianting Committee publication, dated July 15, 2008.

complexity, increasing our understanding of ASD requires new knowledge from various fields of study such as neuroscience, genetics, immunology, biology, psychology, and pharmacology.

To identify the most significant scientific advances in these and other relevant fields in calendar year 2007, the NIMH Autism Team asked senior leaders and program contacts at nine federal agencies and 10 private organizations that fund ASD research (see Appendix A on page 20 for a listing) to identify significant ASD research accomplishments supported by their organizations during 2007 and to identify the peer-reviewed article(s) that report the accomplishment. Fifteen organizations responded to the request.

In addition, the NIH Library searched for relevant primary reports in peer-reviewed journals and for reports featured in the news sections of journals such as *Science* or *Nature*, in publications dedicated to disseminating highlights from scientific journals (*Science News*), and in the news section of the NIH consumer health website (Medline Plus).

To be considered, scientific findings must have been published (or e-published) in calendar year 2007 in peer-reviewed journals or the Center for Disease Control and Prevention's Morbidity and Mortality Weekly Report.

When available, previous or subsequent research (i.e., published before or after calendar year 2007) provided additional information or context. Approximately 140 publications from over 50 peer-reviewed journals were considered for inclusion. The following summary of 54 publications is intended to highlight some of the areas where critical advances were made in the past year.

For individuals and families affected by ASD, the most meaningful research findings may be ones that address six critical questions they face:

- When should I be concerned?
- How can I understand what is happening?
- What caused this to happen, and can this be prevented?
- Which treatments and interventions will help?
- Where can I turn for services?
- What does the future hold?

This report highlights ten scientific advances in ASD research from 2007, organized by these critical questions faced by individuals and families affected by ASD.

KEY ADVANCES IN ASD RESEARCH IN 2007

When should I be concerned?

- *ASD Diagnosis May Be Possible Soon After First Birthday*

How can I understand what is happening?

- Brain Anatomy Holds Clues to ASD
- Deficits in Processing Information from Faces May Disrupt Social Interaction
- Immune System May Play Role in Prenatal Brain Development Unusual Head Growth Is Associated with ASD

What caused this to happen, and can this be prevented?

- Changes in Many Different Genes Contribute to Autism Research on Model Organisms Helps Clarify Gene Function

Which treatments and interventions will help?

- Interventions Can Reduce ASD Symptoms Substantially

Where can I turn for services?

- Multistate Survey Confirms High Prevalence of ASD

What does the future hold?

- Autism Costs U.S. Society More Than $35 Billion Per Year

WHEN SHOULD I BE CONCERNED?

ASD Diagnosis May Be Possible Soon after First Birthday

Most cases of autism and related disorders are not diagnosed until after a child's third birthday. Yet early intervention can have a critical influence on the future course of ASD. With the American Academy of Pediatrics recently issuing clinical reports that call for systematic early screening for autism, a number of reports in 2007 focused on how to accurately detect or rule out autism and related disorders early in life.

One study tracked social and communication skills from ages 14 months to 36 months in 107 infants who had an older sibling with ASD and therefore were at higher risk for the disorder.[1] The study also tracked 18 low-risk healthy controls from unaffected families. By the end of the study, 30 of the high-risk children were diagnosed with ASD.

Half of these 30 children exhibited marked signs of disturbed sociability and play behavior by 14 months. They rarely initiated communications or shared experiences with others, missed social cues, used toys inappropriately, and displayed a limited repertoire of words and gestures. In contrast to this early-diagnosis group, a later-diagnosis group showed a very different course. At 14 months, they were distinguishable from healthy children only in that they shifted their gaze less between objects and a person's eyes. However, their social functioning subsequently deteriorated so that by their second birthday, these children behaved similarly to the early-diagnosis group.

This study concluded that about half of all children with ASD can be diagnosed soon after their first birthday. Others with the disorder appear to develop normally until that age and then falter or regress during their second year. Testing for ASD therefore has to occur at different times to detect varying patterns of onset.

Relatively simple tests can provide valuable information. In one study, 100 percent of children who developed normally responded to their name on the first or second call when they were 12 months old.[2] Most of the children at high-risk of ASD also responded. But three-fourths of the children who failed the task were identified as having developmental problems when they reached 24 months of age. This test does not identify all children at risk of developmental problems, since some children with developmental delays still responded to their name at 12 months, but failing to respond to name is highly suggestive of a developmental abnormality.

In some cases, even earlier detection may be possible. One project studied 31 infant siblings of children with autism and 24 comparison infants at 6 months of age by monitoring the movements of their eyes during a social interaction with a caregiver.[3]

Ten of the eleven infants who failed the test had an older sibling with autism. While failing this test does not warrant a diagnosis, it can identify subgroups of infants who need further assessment.

Because the younger siblings of children with ASD are more likely to develop ASD than are other children, focusing on them enables more targeted and efficient studies.[4] However, some types of autism may run in families, while other cases appear sporadically. Studying the younger siblings of children with ASD may reveal more about the familial forms of autism than about the sporadic cases.

Several important studies assessed the reliability of the techniques used to diagnose ASD. For example, evaluation of the Social Communication Questionnaire revealed that it is helpful in identifying children with developmental problems who require more specific assessment for autism and related disorders.[5,6] Studies of other diagnostic tools demonstrated that they generally produce the same diagnoses at different points in a child's life.[7] A separate investigation, however, showed that 13 out of 73 children who received an ASD diagnosis at approximately 2 years of age lost the diagnosis when reassessed at approximately 4 years of age, though the reasons for this are unknown.[8]

How Can I Understand What Is Happening?

Brain Anatomy Holds Clues to ASD

The development of sophisticated magnetic resonance imaging (MRI) methods has given researchers the ability to accurately visualize many aspects of brain structure.

The result has been a wealth of provocative findings about the anatomy and interconnections of brain regions in people with ASD.

One study examined the brain anatomy of 14 adult women with ASD.[9] They tended to have a larger density of white matter in particular regions of the brain (i.e., bilaterally in the fronto-parietal, posterior temporal lobes, and the cerebellum) than did people without ASD. They also tended to have a significantly reduced density of gray matter in the fronto-temporal cortices and limbic system and of white matter in the anterior temporal lobes. Furthermore, the less gray matter they had in the right limbic regions of the brain, the greater their communication deficits.

Though these findings are in adults and may differ substantially from patterns in children, they replicate previous findings in adult males. They also point to specific alterations in white matter densities that are associated with specific symptoms of autism.

Another study found that young children with ASD who have cognitive deficits have characteristically shaped hippocampi, a part of the brain involved in memory and spatial navigation.[10] Furthermore, these alterations in hippocampal shape are correlated with the degree of the children's cognitive deficits.

Functional MRI (fMRI) can reveal which parts of the brain are active while individuals are performing specific physical or mental tasks. A group of high-functioning participants with autism was compared with a control group as they both performed a task that engages spatial and executive reasoning.[11] The group with autism displayed several distinct indications of reduced connectivity in their brains. For example, the synchronization of activity between different parts of the brain (i.e., frontal and parietal areas of activation) was lower for participants with autism than participants in the control group.

Measures of brain waves demonstrated a difference in connectivity among brain regions in individuals living with ASD.[12,13] Investigations of the relative sizes and functions of brain regions also revealed a disparity in brain connectivity.[14]

All of these findings have contributed to a hypothesis that ASD occurs when parts of the brain involved in complex functions are not optimally connected during development.[15]

This hypothesis, which is now being intensively investigated, could account for many of the behavioral features seen in ASD, as well as for the timing of their emergence.

Deficits in Processing Information from Faces May Disrupt Social Interaction

Many children and adults with ASD perceive and analyze the visual information conveyed by facial expression differently than do other people. They look at and attend to faces in a different way, tending to avoid eye contact with others and scan parts of the face in atypical patterns.[16] Functional imaging of their brains shows that the neural regions involved in face processing are less active in social situations.

Some unaffected family members of people with ASD share these traits. In one study, the siblings (8 – 18 years of age) of children with ASD were, like the children with ASD, less likely to fix their gaze on the eyes of others, and they tended to have less than average brain activity in face-processing regions.[17]

Also, the volume of the amygdala, a part of the brain involved in processing and remembering emotions, was diminished in the unaffected siblings and the children with ASD, compared to other people.

In another study of adults, 13 with either high-functioning autism or Asperger's syndrome and 13 controls, brain imaging was done while the study participants looked at fearful faces.[18] The portions of the brain involved in processing emotions showed greater activation in the adults unaffected by autism or Asperger's syndrome. Also, as the facial expressions became more fearful, the activation of the brain increased for the unaffected adults, but stayed the same for the group with autism or Asperger's syndrome.

Deficits in processing information from faces may lead to persistent social deficits in individuals with ASD, even among those with an IQ and vocabulary in the normal range. For example, the pragmatic (social) aspects of language pose difficulties for people with ASD who are otherwise quite verbal. Interestingly, it has been shown that the activity of key brain regions in children with ASD that underlie these difficulties may be improved. In a study that used the comprehension of irony (an aspect of pragmatic language) as an assessment tool, explicit instructions to pay attention to facial expression and tone of voice created greater brain activity in 18 boys with ASD.[19] If this could translate into better functioning in social situations, interventions might be developed to help individuals with ASD who have pragmatic language difficulties.

These and other findings about brain activity during face processing may provide valuable clues about the origins and mechanisms of differences in social interaction observed in ASD. They may also point toward the development of interventions that could help those with ASD interact with others more easily.

Immune System May Play Role in Prenatal Brain Development

Over the past several years, a number of hypotheses about how the immune system might contribute to autism and other neurodevelopmental disorders such as schizophrenia, Tourette's syndrome, and obsessive compulsive disorder have emerged.

Although research has not yielded clear or definitive answers to the question of immune involvement, some recent findings suggest that the immune systems of parents and their children may affect early brain development and the onset and fluctuation of symptoms in some children with ASD.

In one study, researchers looked at blood samples from 61 mothers whose children have autism and at samples from a control group of 62 mothers whose children were developing typically.[20] They isolated antibodies, proteins produced as part of the immune response, from the blood samples and exposed the antibodies to an array of fetal brain proteins. Antibodies from seven of the 61 samples from the autism group reacted with two clusters of fetal brain proteins, while none of the samples from the mothers in the control group produced this result.

There was no similar reaction when maternal antibodies were exposed to adult brain proteins. Though more work will be necessary to identify the specific fetal brain proteins involved, these early results suggest that in some cases maternal immune molecules could interfere with normal brain development. The reaction was most common in the mothers of children with the regressive form of autism, which is characterized by the loss of social or language skills after a period of typical development.

In another study, blood samples were collected from 11 mothers and their children with autism, from women and their children without a history of autism, and from children with other neurodevelopmental disorders. These samples then were exposed to a large number of brain proteins derived from prenatal, postnatal, and adult rats.[21]

The blood samples from the children with autism, their mothers, and the children with other neurodevelopmental disorders had consistent patterns of reactions to prenatal, but not postnatal or adult, brain proteins, a finding that was not observed in the samples from mothers and children with no history of autism. The proteins producing these reactions were not identified.

In a study of rhesus monkeys, four pregnant rhesus monkeys were exposed to antibodies collected from mothers of children with ASD.[22] The behavior of their offspring was compared to the behavior of four monkeys exposed prenatally to antibodies from mothers of typically developing children and five untreated monkeys. The monkeys exposed prenatally to antibodies from mothers of children with autism were more hyperactive and demonstrated more whole-body repetitive behaviors than the monkeys exposed to antibodies from mothers of typically developing children or untreated monkeys.

If the transfer of specific antibodies from a mother to a developing fetus is a risk factor for autism, treatments might be devised that could prevent development of ASD in some children.

Unusual Head Growth Is Associated with ASD

Many, but not all, children with ASD have periods of unusual head growth during their first few years of life. In 2007, studies began to link this observation with specific mechanisms of brain development.

Longitudinal investigations of children at risk for ASD have improved the understanding of when altered head growth occurs and how it is related to symptoms.

In one study, researchers analyzed the head measurements of 28 boys who developed autism -- 17 with early onset, and 11 with regressive features -- from birth to age three.[23] Until about twelve months of age, the heads of the children later diagnosed with autism grew faster than typically developing children. After the twelve-month mark, rates of head growth became more variable and did not differ overall from those of typically developing children.

The period of accelerated growth precedes and overlaps with the onset of symptoms, while the period of normal growth coincides with a worsening of symptoms in the second year of life.

Investigators are trying to understand the cause of this atypical pattern of head growth. Previous MRI studies had shown that children with ASD have a larger volume of white matter in particular parts of their brain, suggesting a link between brain volume and head growth. A 2007 study revealed that children with autism who have increased white matter also have poorer motor skills, marking the first time that white matter volume has been linked with functional impairment in children with autism.[24]

Another study showed that having a particular version of a gene that influences serotonin in the brain is associated with the volume of the brain's gray matter.[25] Some evidence suggests that levels of serotonin in the brain can influence brain growth and connections between neurons, which could connect the gene variants, altered brain growth, and autism.

Continued research is needed to understand the cause and significance of unusual brain and head growth in some children with autism. Studies that track children over many years are critical to better understand head growth as a potential biomarker for ASD. Many children who develop typically have larger than normal heads. But pediatricians may be able to monitor head growth in infants at risk of autism, such as those who have family members with ASD.

Detection of unusual head growth, combined with other risk factors, may provide a means for early identification and treatment.

What Caused this to Happen, and Can This be Prevented?

Changes in Many Different Genes Contribute to Autism

In 2007, several teams of researchers made major discoveries of specific genetic changes that contribute to ASD. While these changes account for just a fraction of ASD cases, they provide valuable clues about the origins of ASD and related disorders. Surprisingly, many of the discoveries involve genetic changes (deletions and duplications of segments of DNA) that have only been recognized as being important in the last few years.

Using new technology that reveals gaps and extra copies in DNA sequences, researchers scanned the DNA of 195 people with ASD and 196 unaffected individuals.[26] They found that 14 of the people with ASD had deletions and duplications of genetic material not found in their parents, while only 2 of the unaffected people had such genetic changes. The genetic deletions and duplications occurred throughout the DNA of the people with ASD, suggesting that changes in many different genes contribute to autism. Several investigations are under way to determine whether these mutations are associated with specific features or subtypes of autism.

These findings have contributed to new hypotheses about the inheritance of ASD. By studying the patterns of inheritance in 145 families, researchers have proposed that two distinct types of genetic changes may contribute to the development of autism.[27] In families with just one affected member, rare, spontaneous deletions and duplications may be a causal factor for some cases of ASD. While these structural changes are genetic, they are not inherited in the classic sense of being passed across multiple generations. In families with more than one affected member, ASD may result from multiple, subtle common variations in DNA sequence passed from a parent to a child. Although further investigation is needed, recent genetic findings suggest that sporadic and familial autism may represent different forms of autism with distinct forms of genetic risk.

By comparing the DNA of people with ASD to that of unaffected individuals, geneticists also have uncovered an increasing number of variations in specific genes that have been linked to ASD and other related disorders. In particular, variations of several genes involved in the formation and function of synapses appear to contribute to the development of ASD. For example, three different groups using entirely different methods replicated a link between autism and variants of a gene on chromosome 7 known as CNTNAP2. In one study, this gene variation was associated with such factors as the age at which boys with autism say their first word.[28,29,30] The gene is one of several synaptic protein genes now linked to ASD. Mice engineered with mutations of some of these same synaptic protein genes manifest reductions in social behavior.[31,32] By understanding the mechanisms that tie specific genes to ASD, researchers may be able to develop interventions to influence brain development during such critical periods as the acquisition of language.

Another critically important genetic region is located on chromosome 16. This region contains genes involved in both the development of the brain and in the functioning of the immune system. In a DNA scan of 1,441 children with ASD, five children were missing a section of chromosome 16 that contains about 25 genes, including genes involved in brain development, and seven had duplicates of the region.[33] Researchers estimate that about one percent of autism cases are caused by spontaneous deletions or duplications of this part of chromosome [16].

While this finding may be important for studies of risk, the changes on chromosome 16 are apparently not specific for autism. A very small percentage of people -- perhaps 0.01 percent -- have the deletion on chromosome 16 but do not have ASD. Other people with the deletion have different developmental disorders, such as attention deficit hyperactivity disorder and schizophrenia. Studies are under way to identify the specific genes associated with ASD and other conditions.

Research on Model Organisms Helps Clarify Gene Function

Creating better drug medications for ASD requires basic scientific research and new animal models to use in the processes of drug discovery and development. In the past year, powerful tools for manipulating the genomes of model animals, particularly mice, have led to considerable progress in understanding the function of genes. This, in turn, may lead to new treatment targets. For example, research in genetically manipulated mice provided some of the most exciting findings of 2007. One of these was the demonstration that neurological deficits in a mouse model of Rett syndrome can be reversed.[34] Rett syndrome is a serious childhood neurological disease that is physically disabling and frequently includes symptoms of autism. Caused by mutations in a gene known as MECP2, the syndrome impairs speech and movement. In these studies, mice engineered to lack a functioning MECP2 gene during development exhibited the symptoms of Rett syndrome. To determine whether their symptoms were reversible or not, they were manipulated so that the gene became functional and then examined to determine whether this manipulation reversed some of the consequences of the gene deletion. The behavioral and cognitive deficits diminished quickly in both immature and mature animals. Efforts are now under way to determine how this finding might be applied to humans, which could lead to a treatment not only for Rett syndrome but potentially for symptoms of autism resulting from other causes.

Another study examined mice that were manipulated to have a genetic defect that mimics the cause of fragile X syndrome in humans, which is the leading identified cause of autism. When an additional genetic manipulation was performed as a correction, the mice exhibited improved brain development and memory, normal body growth, and fewer seizures.[35] Drugs designed to perform this same type of correction are now undergoing clinical trials as a way of treating symptoms of fragile X syndrome and possibly related disorders, including ASD.

Other mouse models have enabled researchers to examine the roles of specific genes and molecules suspected of being involved in some cases of ASD.[36,37,38] Several of these genes are involved in the growth of brain cells and establishing connections among them during brain development, processes that appear to be closely linked with the origins of autism.[39]

Several 2007 studies reported on the development of mouse strains that exhibit many of the features of autism in humans, including abnormal social interactions, deficits in communication, and high levels of repetitive behaviors.[40] For example, one strain displays low levels of social interaction and marked resistance to change.[41] Such mouse strains can be studied to discover the genetic changes that cause these characteristics. They also can be used to examine the role of environmental toxins in triggering ASD, better pinpoint the brain mechanisms involved in such triggers, and thereby assist in developing potential new treatments for ASD.

Which Treatments and Interventions will Help?

Interventions Can Reduce ASD Symptoms Substantially

Behavioral and pharmacological interventions can substantially reduce the symptoms of autism. In the past year, important progress has been made in testing new interventions and assessing the efficacy of existing interventions.

Behavioral treatments have been studied extensively and shown to be efficacious in improving symptoms of autism. A recent study compared children who began intensive behavioral therapy between the ages of 4 and 7 with a comparison group of children who received a community treatment involving aspects of several treatment models.[42] The intensive behavioral treatment group showed larger increases in IQ and adaptive functioning than the comparison group. The behavioral treatment group also displayed fewer aberrant behaviors and social problems at follow-up. Another project showed that providing families with a home-based behavioral program in addition to a center-based program improved cognitive development and behavior in young children with autism and developmental delay.[43] The improvements were especially marked for children from families with high levels of stress.

The Picture Exchange Communication System (PECS) is a training package that teaches children and adults with autism and other communication deficits to initiate communication.

It is widely used in community settings for children with autism but has received little empirical testing. In one recent study, children between ages 3 and 7 who received 15 hours of PECS teaching over five weeks initiated communication and interacted with others much better than did a group that did not receive PECS teaching.[44] Further evaluation is still warranted, as this was not a randomized trial.

In 2006, risperidone became the first FDA-approved pharmacologic therapy for certain symptoms of autism. First introduced in 1993 as medication used to treat symptoms of schizophrenia, risperidone has now been shown to be effective as a treatment of irritability associated with autistic disorder in children and adolescents aged 5-16 years. A randomized, double-blind, placebo-controlled trial demonstrated in 2007 that risperidone significantly improved severe behavioral problems associated with autism such as tantrums, aggression, and self-injurious behavior.[45] However, a review article called for larger and longer-term studies of the drug's benefits and possible adverse effects.[46]

Other pharmacological and biological treatments are being explored, although they are all in the early phases of study and conclusions cannot yet be made about efficacy or possible adverse side effects. Results from small studies are often not confirmed in larger trials, and sometimes side effects emerge with increased numbers of subjects.

Preliminary findings from small studies need replication in randomized, controlled trials with larger samples before any recommendations about their use can be made. Examples include:

- A small randomized, double-blind, placebo-controlled 6-week trial with 13 children and adolescents with autism reported that omega-3 fatty acids outperformed placebo in terms of reducing hyperactivity and stereotypy.[47]
- In another randomized, double-blind, placebo-controlled crossover trial, 15 adults diagnosed with autism or related disorders were given oxytocin, a hormone that can enhance the ability to interpret subtle social clues.[48] All were better able to judge whether speech was happy, indifferent, angry, or sad after receiving the hormone.
- A medication of interest is memantine, which antagonizes certain actions of multiple brain neurotransmitters. In an open-label study, 151 patients with prior diagnoses of autism or pervasive developmental disorder not otherwise specified took memantine, in addition to other treatments already prescribed, over a 21-month period.[49] Significant improvements were seen in language function, social behavior, and self-stimulatory behaviors, though the latter improved to a lesser degree than did language and behavior.
- Pioglitazone exerts an anti-inflammatory effect in brain cells suspected of being involved in some cases of ASD and is used to treat type 2 diabetes. In an open-label case series of 25 children with ASD, the medication is reported to have produced significant decreases in irritability, lethargy, stereotypy, and hyperactivity.[50] Younger children showed the most dramatic effects.

Where Can I Turn for Services?

Multistate Survey Confirms High Prevalence of ASD

The most thorough survey ever done of the prevalence of ASD (i.e., the proportion of affected individuals at a given point in time) estimated that between one in 100 to one in 300 -- with an average of one in every 150 children (for study years 2002 and 2004) -- may have the disorder.[51]

With the completion of additional study years (2006 and 2008 are underway), this effort will provide important information about autism trends in the United States.

The investigators looked at children aged eight years old in 2002 in 14 areas of the United States. They examined evaluation records at health facilities at all 14 sites and evaluations for special education services at 10 of the 14 sites. Children with behaviors consistent with autistic disorder, pervasive developmental disorder not otherwise specified, or Asperger's syndrome were classified as having ASD.

Of 407,578 children in the 14 sites, 2,685 (0.66 percent) were classified as having ASD. The prevalence per 1,000 children ranged from 3.3 per 1,000 in Alabama to 10.6 in New Jersey, with the majority of sites ranging from 5.2 to 7.6.

The overall mean of 6.6 per 1,000 children means that one child in every 150 across all sites was identified as having ASD. While all sites used a rigorous, consistent method for data collection and case determination, sites varied in their ability to ascertain ASD cases. For example, the average prevalence of ASD among sites that relied solely on review of health records (4 sites including Alabama) was significantly lower than that of sites that were able to review both health and education records (10 sites including New Jersey).

The majority of the children surveyed were receiving special education services at age eight.

A majority also had a documented history of concerns regarding their development before age three. However, the median age at which they were diagnosed with ASD ranged from 49 months in Utah to 66 months in Alabama. The ratio of males to females ranged from 3.4 to 1 in three states to 6.5 to 1 in Utah.

For six of the sites, prevalence data were also available for 2000.[52] In four of the sites, the prevalence rate was stable. In Georgia it increased 17 percent, and in West Virginia it increased 39 percent.

The data establish a baseline for tracking trends over time, and continuation of the project in the re-funded sites will shed light on whether the prevalence of ASD is changing.

A separate study from Denmark revealed a rising incidence of ASD.[53] Incidence refers to the number of new cases over time in the same population. It examined the health records of all 669,995 children born in Denmark from 1990 through 1999 and found statistically significant increases in the incidence of ASD, hyperkinetic disorder, and Tourette's syndrome.

The investigators found no significant change in the incidence of obsessive-compulsive disorder across birth years. The study concluded that increases in ASD might be part of a more widespread increase in neurologic disorders, though it was not possible to determine the reasons for the change.

WHAT DOES THE FUTURE HOLD?

Autism Costs U.S. Society More Than $35 Billion per Year

Autism is a very expensive disorder. A previous study found that ASD costs U.S. society more than $35 billion each year. A recent follow-up study elaborated on this finding, reporting that the incremental costs to society of ASD are $3.2 million per person with ASD over a lifetime, and that the annual costs are greater for adults with ASD than for children.[54]

The costs of autism are both direct and indirect. Direct costs are a measure of the value of the goods and services used to care for those with ASD, while indirect costs are a measure of the value of productivity lost due to ASD. Direct medical costs include those for physicians and other professionals, hospital and emergency department services, drugs, equipment and other supplies, and medically related travel and time.

Direct nonmedical costs include those for special education, transportation, child care and babysitting, respite care, out-of-home placement, home and vehicle modifications, and supported employment services. Indirect costs include the value of lost or impaired work time, benefits, and household services of individuals with ASD and their caregivers because of missed time at work, reduced work hours, switching to a lower-paying but more flexible job, or leaving the workforce.

Direct medical costs are quite high for the first five years of life, averaging around $35,000 per year. They start to decline substantially by age eight years, to about $6,000 per year, and continue to decline through the end of life to around $1,000 annually.

Direct non-medical costs range from $10,000 to approximately $16,000 during the first 20 years of life, peak in the 23- to 27-year age range at around $27,500, and then decline steadily with age to around $8,000 annually. Indirect costs follow a similar non-linear pattern, decreasing from around $43,000 in early life to approximately $36,000 in the 18- to 22-year age range, peaking at ages 23 to 27 years at around $52,000, and then declining through the end of life.

Information on the distribution of costs across a lifetime can help allocate scarce resources to support individuals with ASD and their families. In particular, the substantial costs incurred by adults with ASD point to the difficulties faced by parents of children with ASD as they plan for the transition of their children into adulthood and for their sustained support as adults.

APPENDIX A - LIST OF CONTACTED FEDERAL AND PRIVATE ORGANIZATIONS THAT FUND ASD RESEARCH

Federal Agencies Contacted

1. Administration for Children and Families
2. Centers for Disease Control and Prevention
3. Centers for Medicare and Medicaid Services
4. Department of Defense
5. Department of Education
6. Health and Human Services Office on Disability
7. Health Resources and Services Administration
8. National Institutes of Health
   - National Center for Complementary and Alternative Medicine
   - National Center for Research Resources
   - National Human Genome Research Institute
   - National Institute on Aging
   - National Institute of Child Health and Human Development
   - National Institute on Deafness and Other Communication Disorders
   - National Institute of Environmental Health Sciences
   - National Institute of Mental Health
   - National Institute of Neurological Disorders and Stroke
   - Office of Portfolio Analysis and Strategic Initiatives
9. Substance Abuse and Mental Health Services Administration

Private Organizations Contacted

1. Autism Consortium
2. Autism Research Institute
3. Autism Society of America
4. Autism Speaks
5. Center for Autism and Related Disorders, Inc.– Based in Tarzana, CA
6. Doug Flutie, Jr. Foundation for Autism
7. Organization for Autism Research
8. The Coalition for SafeMinds (Sensible Action For Ending Mercury-Induced Neurological Disorders)

9. The Simons Foundation
10. Southwest Autism Research and Resource Center

End Notes

[1] Landa RJ, Holman KC, Garrett-Mayer E. Social and communication development in toddlers with early and later diagnosis of autism spectrum disorders. Arch Gen Psychiatry. 2007 Jul;64(7):853-64.

[2] Nadig AS, Ozonoff S, Young GS, Rozga A, Sigman M, Rogers Si A prospective study of response to name in infants at risk for autism. Arch Pediatr Adolesc Med. 2007 Apr;161(4):378-83.

[3] Merin N, Young GS, Ozonoff S, Rogers SJ. Visual fixation patterns during reciprocal social interaction distinguish a subgroup of 6-month-old infants at-risk for autism from comparison infants. J Autism Dev Disord. 2007 Jan;37(1):108-21.

[4] Stone WL, McMahon CR, Yoder PJ, Walden TA. Early social-communicative and cognitive development of younger siblings of children with autism spectrum disorders. Arch Pediatr Adolesc Med. 2007 Apr;161(4):384-90.

[5] Allen CW, Silove N, Williams K, Hutchins P. Validity of the social communication questionnaire in assessing risk of autism in preschool children with developmental problems. J Autism Dev Disord. 2007 Aug;37(7):1272-8.

[6] Chandler S, Charman T, Baird G, Simonoff E, Loucas T, Meldrum D, Scott M, Pickles A. Validation of the social communication questionnaire in a population cohort of children with autism spectrum disorders. J Am Acad Child Adolesc Psychiatry. 2007 Oct;46(10):1324-32.

[7] Chawarska K, Klin A, Paul R, Volkmar F. Autism spectrum disorder in the second year: stability and change in syndrome expression. J Child Psychol Psychiatry. 2007 Feb;48(2):128-38.

[8] Sutera S, Pandey J, Esser EL, Rosenthal MA, Wilson LB, Barton M, Green J, Hodgson S, Robins DL, Dumont-Mathieu T, Fein D. Predictors of optimal outcome in toddlers diagnosed with autism spectrum disorders. J Autism Dev Disord. 2007 Jan;37(1):98-107.

[9] Craig MC, Zaman SH, Daly EM, Cutter WJ, Robertson DM, Hallahan B, Toal F, Reed S, Ambikapathy A, Brammer M, Murphy CM, Murphy DG. Women with autistic-spectrum disorder: magnetic resonance imaging study of brain anatomy. Br J Psychiatry. 2007 Sep;191:224-8.

[10] Dager SR, Wang L, Friedman SD, Shaw DW, Constantino JN, Artru AA, Dawson G, Csernansky JG. Shape mapping of the hippocampus in young children with autism spectrum disorder. AJNR Am J Neuroradiol. 2007 Apr;28(4):672-7.

[11] Just MA, Cherkassky VL, Keller TA, Kana RK, Minshew NJ. Functional and anatomical cortical underconnectivity in autism: evidence from an fMRI study of an executive function task and corpus callosum morphometry. Cereb Cortex. 2007 Apr;17(4):951-61.

[12] Murias M, Webb SJ, Greenson J, Dawson G. Resting state cortical connectivity reflected in EEG coherence in individuals with autism. Biol Psychiatry. 2007 Aug 1;62(3):270-3.

[13] Wilson TW, Rojas DC, Reite ML, Teale PD, Rogers SJ. Children and adolescents with autism exhibit reduced MEG steady-state gamma responses. Biol Psychiatry. 2007 Aug 1;62(3):192-7.

[14] Neeley ES, Bigler ED, Krasny L, Ozonoff S, McMahon W, Lainhart JE. Quantitative temporal lobe differences: autism distinguished from controls using classification and regression tree analysis. Brain Dev. 2007 Aug;29(7):389-99.

[15] Geschwind DH, Levitt P. Autism spectrum disorders: developmental disconnection syndromes. Curr Opin Neurobiol. 2007 Feb;17(1):103-11.

[16] Spezio ML, Adolphs R, Hurley RS, Piven J. Analysis of face gaze in autism using "Bubbles". Neuropsychologia. 2007 Jan 7;45(1):144-51.

[17] Dalton KM, Nacewicz BM, Alexander AL, Davidson RJ. Gaze-fixation, brain activation, and amygdala volume in unaffected siblings of individuals with autism. Biol Psychiatry. 2007 Feb 15;61(4):512-20.

[18] Ashwin C, Baron-Cohen S, Wheelwright S, O'Riordan M, Bullmore ET. Differential activation of the amygdala and the 'social brain' during fearful face-processing in Asperger Syndrome. Neuropsychologia. 2007 Jan 7;45(1):2-14.

[19] Wang AT, Lee SS, Sigman M, Dapretto M. Reading affect in the face and voice: neural correlates of interpreting communicative intent in children and adolescents with autism spectrum disorders. Arch Gen Psychiatry. 2007 Jun;64(6):698-708.

[20] Braunschweig D, Ashwood P, Krakowiak P, Hertz-Picciotto I, Hansen R, Croen LA, Pessah IN, Van de Water J. Autism: Maternally derived antibodies specific for fetal brain proteins. Neurotoxicology. 2008 Mar;29(2):226-231. Epub 12/15/07.

[21] Zimmerman AW, Connors SL, Matteson KJ, Lee LC, Singer HS, Castaneda JA, Pearce DA. Maternal antibrain antibodies in autism. Brain Behav Immun. 2007 Mar;21(3):351-7.

[22] Martin LA, Ashwood P, Braunschweig D, Cabanlit M, Van de Water J, Amaral DG. Stereotypies and hyperactivity in rhesus monkeys exposed to IgG from mothers of children with autism. Brain Behav. Immun. 2008 Feb 7 [Epub].

[23] Dawson G, Munson J, Webb SJ, Nalty T, Abbott R, Toth K. Rate of head growth decelerates and symptoms worsen in the second year of life in autism. Biol Psychiatry. 2007 Feb 15;61(4):458-64.

[24] Mostofsky SH, Burgess MP, Gidley Larson JC. Increased motor cortex white matter volume predicts motor impairment in autism. Brain. 2007 Aug;130(Pt 8):2117-22.

[25] Wassink TH, Hazlett HC, Epping EA, Arndt S, Dager SR, Schellenberg GD, Dawson G, Piven J. Cerebral cortical gray matter overgrowth and functional variation of the serotonin transporter gene in autism. Arch Gen Psychiatry. 2007 Jun;64(6):709-17.

[26] Sebat J, Lakshmi B, Malhotra D, Troge J, Lese-Martin C, Walsh T, Yamrom B, Yoon S, Krasnitz A, Kendall J, Leotta A, Pai D, Zhang R, Lee YH, Hicks J, Spence SJ, Lee AT, Puura K, Lehtimäki T, Ledbetter D, Gregersen PK, Bregman J, Sutcliffe JS, Jobanputra V, Chung W, Warburton D, King MC, Skuse D, Geschwind DH, Gilliam TC, Ye K, Wigler M., Strong association of de novo copy number mutations with autism. Science. 2007 Apr 20;316(5823):445-9.

[27] Zhao X, Leotta A, Kustanovich V, Lajonchere C, Geschwind DH, Law K, Law P, Qiu S, Lord C, Sebat J, Ye K, Wigler M. A unified genetic theory for sporadic and inherited autism. Proc Natl Acad Sci USA. 2007 Jul 31;104(31):12831-6.

[28] Alarcón M, Abrahams BS, Stone JL, Duvall JA, Perederiy JV, Bomar JM, Sebat J, Wigler M, Martin CL, Ledbetter DH, Nelson SF, Cantor RM, Geschwind DH. Linkage, association, and gene-expression analyses identify CNTNAP2 as an autism-susceptibility gene. Am J Hum Genet. 2008 Jan;82(1):150-9.

[29] Arking DE, Cutler DJ, Brune CW, Teslovich TM, West K, Ikeda M, Rea A, Guy M, Lin S, Cook EH, Chakravarti A. A common genetic variant in the neurexin superfamily member CNTNAP2 increases familial risk of autism. Am J Hum Genet. 2008 Jan;82(1):160-4.

[30] Bakkaloglu B, O'Roak BJ, Louvi A, Gupta AR, Abelson JF, Morgan TM, Chawarska K, Klin A, ErcanSencicek AG, Stillman AA, Tanriover G, Abrahams BS, Duvall JA, Robbins EM, Geschwind DH, Biederer T, Gunel M, Lifton RP, State MW. Molecular cytogenetic analysis and resequencing of contactin associated protein-like 2 in autism spectrum disorders. Am J Hum Genet. 2008 Jan;82(1):165-73.

[31] Tabuchi K, Blundell J, Etherton MR, Hammer RE, Liu, X Powell CM, Südhof TC. A Neuroligin-3 mutation implicated in autism increases inhibitory synaptic transmission in mice. Science 2007 Oct 5; 318(5827):71-76

[32] Jamain S, Radyushkin K, Hammerschmidt K, Boretius S, Varoqueaux F Ramanantsoa N, Gallego J, Ronnenberg A, Winter D, Frahm J, Fischer J, Bourgeron T, Ehrenreich H, and Brose N. Reduced social interaction and ultrasonic communication in a mouse model of monogenic heritable autism. PNAS 2008 Feb 5;105(5):1710-1715.

[33] Weiss LA, Shen Y, Korn JM, Arking DE, Miller DT, Fossdal R, Saemundsen E, Stefansson H, Ferreira MA, Green T, Platt OS, Ruderfer DM, Walsh CA, Altshuler D, Chakravarti A, Tanzi RE, Stefansson K, Santangelo SL, Usella JF, Sklar P, Wu BL, Daly MJ; Autism Consortium. Association between microdeletion and microduplication at 16p11.2 and autism. N Engl J Med. 2008 Feb 14;358(7):667-75.

[34] Guy J, Gan J, Selfridge J, Cobb S, Bird A. Reversal of neurological defects in a mouse model of Rett syndrome. Science. 2007 Feb 23;315(5815):1143-7.

[35] Dölen G, Osterweil E, Rao BS, Smith GB, Auerbach BD, Chattarji S, Bear MF. Correction of fragile X syndrome in mice. Neuron. 2007 Dec 20;56(6):955-62.

[36] Sadakata T, Kakegawa W, Mizoguchi A, Washida M, Katoh-Semba R, Shutoh F, Okamoto T, Nakashima H, Kimura K, Tanaka M, Sekine Y, Itohara S, Yuzaki M, Nagao S, Furuichi T. Impaired cerebellar development and function in mice lacking CAPS2, a protein involved in neurotrophin release. J Neurosci. 2007 Mar 7;27(10):2472-82.

[37] Tabuchi K, Blundell J, Etherton MR, Hammer RE, Liu X, Powell CM, Südhof TC. A neuroligin-3 mutation implicated in autism increases inhibitory synaptic transmission in mice. Science. 2007 Oct 5;318(5847):71-6.

[38] Chubykin AA, Atasoy D, Etherton MR, Brose N, Kavalali ET, Gibson JR, Südhof TC. Activity- dependent validation of excitatory versus inhibitory synapses by neuroligin-1 versus neuroligin-2. Neuron. 2007 Jun 21;54(6):919-31.

[39] Autism Genome Project Consortium et al. Mapping autism risk loci using genetic linkage and chromosomal rearrangements. Nat Genet. 2007 Mar;39(3):319-28.

[40] Crawley JN. Mouse behavioral assays relevant to the symptoms of autism. Brain Pathol. 2007 Oct;17(4):448-59.

[41] Moy SS, Nadler JJ, Young NB, Perez A, Holloway LP, Barbaro RP, Barbaro JR, Wilson LM, Threadgill DW, Lauder JM, Magnuson TR, Crawley JN. Mouse behavioral tasks relevant to autism: phenotypes of 10 inbred strains. Behav Brain Res. 2007 Jan 10;176(1):4-20.

[42] Eikeseth S, Smith T, Jahr E, Eldevik S. Outcome for children with autism who began intensive behavioral treatment between ages 4 and 7: a comparison controlled study. Behav Modif. 2007 May;31(3):264-78.

[43] Rickards AL, Walstab JE, Wright-Rossi RA, Simpson J, Reddihough DS. A randomized, controlled trial of a home-based intervention program for children with autism and developmental delay. J Dev Behav Pediatr. 2007 Aug;28(4):308-16.

[44] Carr D, Felce J. The effects of PECS teaching to Phase III on the communicative interactions between children with autism and their teachers. J Autism Dev Disord. 2007 Apr;37(4):724-37.

[45] Pandina GJ, Bossie CA, Youssef E, Zhu Y, Dunbar F. Risperidone improves behavioral symptoms in children with autism in a randomized, double-blind, placebo-controlled trial. J Autism Dev Disord. 2007 Feb;37(2):367-73.

[46] Jesner OS, Aref-Adib M, Coren E. Risperidone for autism spectrum disorder. Cochrane Database Syst Rev. 2007 Jan 24;(1):CD005040.

[47] Amminger GP, Berger GE, Schäfer MR, Klier C, Friedrich MH, Feucht M. Omega-3 fatty acids supplementation in children with autism: a double-blind randomized, placebo-controlled pilot study. Biol Psychiatry. 2007 Feb 15;61(4):551-3.

[48] Hollander E, Bartz J, Chaplin W, Phillips A, Sumner J, Soorya L, Anagnostou E, Wasserman S. Oxytocin increases retention of social cognition in autism. Biol Psychiatry. 2007 Feb 15;61(4):498-503.

[49] Chez MG, Burton Q, Dowling T, Chang M, Khanna P, Kramer C. Memantine as adjunctive therapy in children diagnosed with autistic spectrum disorders: an observation of initial clinical response and maintenance tolerability. J Child Neurol. 2007 May;22(5):574-9.

[50] Boris M, Kaiser CC, Goldblatt A, Elice MW, Edelson SM, Adams JB, Feinstein DL. Effect of pioglitazone treatment on behavioral symptoms in autistic children. J Neuroinflammation. 2007 Jan 5;4:3.

[51] Autism and Developmental Disabilities Monitoring Network Surveillance Year 2002 Principal Investigators; Centers for Disease Control and Prevention. Prevalence of autism spectrum disorders--autism and developmental disabilities monitoring network, 14 sites, United States, 2002. MMWR Surveill Summ. 2007 Feb 9;56(1):12-28.

[52] Autism and Developmental Disabilities Monitoring Network Surveillance Year 2000 Principal Investigators; Centers for Disease Control and Prevention. Prevalence of autism spectrum disorders--autism and developmental disabilities monitoring network, six sites, United States, 2000. MMWR Surveill Summ. 2007 Feb 9;56(1):1-11.

[53] Atladóttir HO, Parner ET, Schendel D, Dalsgaard S, Thomsen PH, Thorsen P. Time trends in reported diagnoses of childhood neuropsychiatric disorders: a Danish cohort study. Arch Pediatr Adolesc Med. 2007 Feb;161(2):193-8.

[54] Ganz ML. The lifetime distribution of the incremental societal costs of autism. Arch Pediatr Adolesc Med. 2007 Apr;161(4):343-9.

In: Advances in Autism Spectrum Disorder ... ISBN: 978-1-62257-058-4
Editors: R. L. Jackson and A. C. Lee

Chapter 2

SUMMARY OF ADVANCES IN AUTISM SPECTRUM DISORDER RESEARCH: CALENDAR YEAR 2008*

Interagency Autism Coordinating Committee

INTRODUCTION

The dramatic increase in the prevalence of autism spectrum disorders (ASD) over the past two decades has spurred research into all aspects of the disorders. Researchers are now doing critical work to understand what causes ASD, how it can be effectively treated, and how to improve the lives of those affected.

ASD includes a range of developmental disorders that share common features including impaired communication skills and social interactions and restricted, repetitive, and stereotyped patterns of behavior. Currently, the Centers for Disease Control and Prevention (CDC) estimates that about 1 in 150 children in the United States has ASD.

In response to the alarming growth in autism diagnoses, Congress passed the Combating Autism Act of 2006 (P.L. 109-416), which established the Interagency Autism Coordinating Committee (IACC) to coordinate all efforts within the U.S. Department of Health and Human Services related to ASD.

* This is an edited, reformatted and augmented version of an Interagency Autism Coordinating Committee publication, dated August 28, 2009.

The Combating Autism Act requires that, in addition to several other key responsibilities, the IACC must prepare an annual summary of advances in autism research.

The 2008 IACC Summary of Advances highlights 37 significant studies on autism spectrum disorder selected by members of the IACC. A bulleted overview of the major findings in 2008 is followed by a more detailed description of the scientific breakthroughs in each category. Information about funding sources and journal impact factor scores is included in a table at the end of the document.

All articles included in the summary appeared in a peer-reviewed journal during calendar year 2008 and were selected from a broad NIH Library search of biomedical literature databases (e.g., PubMed, Scopus), news sections of major journals (e.g. *Science, Nature*), and publications that highlight findings from scientific journals (e.g., *Science News*).

Articles were also collected from databases of ratings and reviews of scientific publications (e.g., Faculty of 1000 Biology, Cochrane Reviews) and references from major newspapers like the *New York Times* and *Washington Post*.

Members of the IACC voted on the contents and classification of the broad article search containing 257 articles before selecting the final articles included in the 2008 Summary of Advances.

This year's advances are sorted into six topic areas that correspond to six critical questions for those affected by ASD:

- Diagnosis: When should I be concerned?
- Biology: How can I understand what is happening?
- Risk Factors: What caused this to happen and can this be prevented?
- Treatment: Which treatments and interventions will help?
- Services: Where can I turn for services?
- Outcomes: What does the future hold?

The IACC Strategic Plan for ASD Research is also structured around these six questions.[1]

Some topic areas contain noticeably more articles than others. This may reflect a lower level of research funding for some topic areas when compared to others.

As a result, there may be fewer significant advances in some areas. Members of the committee have expressed the hope that increased funding in these areas will lead to more scientific breakthroughs in the future.

Overview of Autism Findings in 2008

Diagnosis: When Should I Be Concerned?

- High-functioning men with ASD show less activity in the brain's cingulate cortex during social interaction. This finding suggests potential for development of new assessment tools.
- General developmental assessments do not detect many children that screen positive on autism-specific assessments. As a result, the authors recommend that all children should be screened using an autism-specific tool. The American Academy of Pediatrics issued a similar recommendation in 2006.

Biology: How Can I Understand What Is Happening?

- The gene associated with Rett syndrome, a pervasive developmental disorder related to autism, is a key regulator of many genes in the hypothalamus. Scientists continue to make discoveries about the complex genetics of ASD and related disorders.
- Genes that cause tuberous sclerosis complex (TSC), a disorder that often co-occurs with autism, have been shown to impair axon formation of neurons.
- Children with autism have greater expression of genes related to the immune system's natural-killer cells compared to typically-developing children. These elevated expression levels could serve as a potential biomarker for diagnosis and suggest the need for further research into the role of the immune system in autism.
- Levels of a specific protein (secreted amyloid precursor protein alpha) are significantly elevated in children with ASD and could also serve as a potential biomarker for the disorder.
- Mothers of children with autism were found to have antibodies in their blood that specifically bind to fetal brain proteins, suggesting that the presence of these antibodies may be associated with a higher risk for autism.
- Measles virus is not found in the bowels of autistic children with gastrointestinal involvement, indicating that the Measles, Mumps, Rubella (MMR) vaccine is not related to autism.

Risk Factors: What Caused This to Happen and Can It Be Prevented?

- Several studies show that changes to the CNTNAP2 gene (Contactin associated protein-like 2), which is thought to play a role in brain cell development and the chemical signaling that enables brain cells to communicate with each other, are linked to ASD.
- Copy number variation (CNV) is emerging as a possible common genetic mechanism that may contribute to the development of autism.
- DNA microdeletions and microduplications (copy number variations) to regions on several chromosomes, including chromosomes 16, 15, and 1, are associated with autism.
- Studying families where parents are related yields clues to the genetic basis of autism.
- Older parents are more likely to have children with ASD.
- Parents who have been hospitalized for a psychiatric disorder are more likely to have children with ASD.
- Births of children with autism show a seasonal pattern.
- Decreased eye contact can be used as a predictor of social impairment in two-year-old children with ASD.

Vaccines

- The majority of evidence does not support a link between vaccines and autism.
- Autism rates in California continued to increase even after thimerosal was removed from nearly all childhood vaccines.
- One study found that children with autism were more likely to have Rh-negative mothers, potentially implicating a thimerosal-containing injection given to mothers with incompatible Rh-factors.

Treatment: Which Treatments and Interventions Will Help?

- The drug rapamycin reduces neurological symptoms in mice with tuberous sclerosis complex, a genetic disorder that often co-occurs with autism. This finding may help to develop effective drug therapies for autism and related developmental disorders.

- A computerized training program improves the ability to process faces for people with ASD.
- Interventions to encourage joint attention and symbolic play are shown to improve language development in preschoolers with ASD.
- Some children with autism have trouble understanding the symbolic nature of pictures. This has implications for users of the Picture Exchange Communication System (PECS) and other picture-based communication.

Services and Supports: Where Can I Turn for Services?

- Children's attitudes about a new classmate with autism are affected by who provides information about the disorder. This suggests that it may be helpful to engage multiple speakers to educate students about autism before mainstreaming a classmate with ASD.
- Medical expenses for children and adolescents with ASD average $3,110 to $6,200 more per year than their typically-developing peers.
- Adding to the financial strain, families of children diagnosed with ASD lose an average of $6,200 or 14 percent of their yearly income. In some cases this is due to one parent leaving the workforce to care for his or her child.

Outcomes: What Does the Future Hold?

- Children with relatively high intelligence, increased receptive language skills, and good verbal and motor imitation are more likely to recover from autism.
- Young autistic children's oral- and manual-motor skills predict later speech fluency.
- Children with better joint attention skills have greater language gains as they get older.
- People with autism are more likely to die from epilepsy and infectious diseases than the general population. Thus, direct care staff could benefit from training to better manage potentially life-threatening physical illnesses that commonly affect people with ASD, in addition to accident prevention.

Diagnosis: When Should I Be Concerned?

Correctly diagnosing children with autism spectrum disorders as early as possible is critical to receiving needed services and interventions. 2 3 4 While the symptoms of autism arise before a child's third birthday, some children are not diagnosed until they are much older. 5 6 Currently there are no biological tests for autism; as a result, children are diagnosed based on a specific set of behavioral criteria outlined in the DSM-IV (Diagnostic and Statistical Manual of Mental Disorders).

Research published in 2008 may help to develop new screening tools for ASD and refine existing diagnostic strategies.

A study investigating the neural activity of people with high-functioning autism during social interactions may lead to new assessment tools. Researchers used functional magnetic resonance imaging (fMRI) to scan the brains of 18 adolescent men with ASD while they played a social exchange game with a partner.[7]

During the game the autistic men showed less activity in the portion of the brain that is used when imagining 'self,' compared to typically developing subjects. The lack of activity in this region, called the cingulate cortex, indicates that some people with high-functioning autism have an impaired ability to recognize 'self' during social situations.

The researchers determined that the cingulate cortex was responsible for modeling 'self' after performing fMRI scans on 81 typically-developing athletes visualizing themselves playing various sports. The scans showed increased blood flow (indicating increased activity) in the cingulate cortex.

After watching the exchange games, the researchers also found that the lack of 'self' response in the brain of the autistic subjects was related to the severity of the person's symptoms. Subjects with more severe autistic symptoms had less activity in the cingulate cortex than did subjects with milder symptoms. This finding may be helpful in developing new diagnostic assessments for ASD.

Another 2008 study identified which screening strategies are most effective for early diagnosis.[8] Many pediatricians use a general developmental assessment for all of their patients and test specifically for autism only after a child shows developmental delays on the general assessment. However, one study found that using the general developmental screening tool, the Parents' Evaluation of Developmental Status (PEDS),[9] did not efficiently screen the majority of children who tested positive on the Modified Checklist for Autism in Toddlers (M-CHAT),[10] an ASDspecific assessment.

During the study, 152 children between the ages of 18 and 30 months were screened using both the PEDS and M-CHAT tools at their well-child visit to their pediatricians. The researchers found that 16 of the 22 children (73%) who tested positive for ASD on the M-CHAT did not show any developmental concerns on the PEDS. These results suggest that the two tools assess different areas of developmental concerns and support the American Academy of Pediatrics recommendations that, in addition to regular developmental screening, children need to be systematically screened starting at 18 months of age using an ASD-specific tool.[11]

Biology: How Can I Understand What Is Happening?

Changes to several genes have been linked to autism spectrum disorders. Better understanding of the biology of these genes and their functions can provide insight into how they contribute to ASD and related disorders.

One gene of interest is MeCP2 (methyl CpG binding protein 2), known to produce a protein essential to normal brain development. Previous studies suggest that MeCP2 is involved in forming connections between brain cells at the synapse -- the junction where communication between neurons occurs. Mutations to the gene can cause Rett Syndrome, a pervasive developmental disorder related to autism, in addition to other disorders of the brain. 12

Recent studies have shown that MeCP2 plays a critical role in activating and repressing genes that direct the activities of neurons in the hypothalamus.[13] After looking at patterns of gene expression in mice that lack MeCP2 and those that overproduce its protein, researchers made an unexpected finding -- MeCP2 activated about 85 percent of the genes of the hypothalamus. These findings show that MeCP2 is a key regulator for many genes in this region of the brain.

Another important finding involved the two genes that cause tuberous sclerosis complex (TSC), TSC1 and TSC2. Tuberous sclerosis complex is a disorder that causes tumor growth and many with the disorder are also diagnosed with epilepsy, mental retardation, and autism. A 2008 study found that the two genes that cause TSC impair the formation of axons,[14] the neuronal projections from the cell body that carry electrical impulses to other cells. The process of axon formation is fundamental to brain development and function. When TSC1 and TSC2 proteins are overexpressed, they suppress axon formation and when lacking, the axon develops abnormally.

Understanding how TSC1 and TSC2 regulate the growth of neurons may help scientists understand TSC and related disorders like autism.

A recent study also noted specific genes that were expressed at higher levels by children with classic autism when compared to typically developing children. The 11 genes that were identified are linked to natural-killer cells,[15] immune cells necessary for mounting the body's defenses against infecting organisms and foreign agents. These findings suggest that certain white blood cell abnormalities seen in children with autism could contribute to the risk of developing the disorder. Researchers also found different patterns of gene expression for children with regressive forms of autism compared to early onset autism, showing that the two may be distinct subtypes of the disorder. There were no genetic differences between children with ASD who had less severe symptoms and typically-developing controls.

Currently there is no single molecular marker that can be used to diagnose autism, but a recent study has found encouraging evidence of a potential biomarker. Researchers found that levels of secreted amyloid precursor protein alpha (sAPP-alpha) were significantly elevated in 60 percent of the children with autism tested.[16] The study, which included 25 autistic children and 25 age-matched controls, found elevated sAPP-alpha levels in children with the ASD. They also found significantly elevated levels of sAPP-alpha in 10 of 150 samples of human umbilical cord blood, showing that elevated sAPP-alpha levels could be measured at birth. Though more research is needed, measuring sAPP-alpha levels in serum and cord blood shows promise for developing an early diagnostic test for ASD.

New findings on the biology of autism also shed light on how reactions of a mother's immune system may contribute to the disorder. A recent study found that mothers of children with autism have immune molecules called antibodies in their circulation that bind to fetal brain proteins in laboratory tests, while mothers of typically developing children do not have similarly-behaving antibodies.[17] The finding of antibodies that bind fetal brain proteins was most common in mothers of children with the regressive form of autism, whose children lose the social and language skills they previously developed. This suggests that the presence of these specific antibodies in the mother's blood confers an elevated risk for having a child with autism.

Researchers isolated antibodies in 61 mothers with autistic children and 62 mothers of typically developing children. Exposing the antibodies to an array of fetal brain proteins revealed that antibodies from seven of the 61 mothers with autistic children reacted with two specific clusters of fetal brain proteins. None of the samples from the mothers in the control group exhibited a response. There was no similar reaction when maternal antibodies were exposed to adult brain proteins, suggesting that these antibodies are specifically targeted toward proteins that are present during fetal development. While outside the scope of this study, the authors hypothesized that these antibodies to fetal brain proteins may somehow be interfering in normal fetal brain development, increasing the risk for autism.

Another study investigating the causation of ASD was unable to show a relationship between the vaccine for measles, mumps, and rubella (MMR) and the onset of autism,[18] as had previously been reported in a 1998 study. The 1998 study had incited public concern after it was reported that autistic children with gastrointestinal (GI) disturbances had measles RNA present in their bowels.[19]

The 2008 study looked at 25 autistic children and 13 typically developing children, all of whom experienced GI disturbances including recurrent abdominal pain, gastroesophageal reflux, vomiting and food allergies. Both groups of children were, on average, five years of age and had received their first MMR vaccination at about 15 months old. The majority of the children in the study had not yet received their second dose of the vaccine. Researchers examined bowel biopsies from the children in the study and found no difference between those with autism and those without -- one of the autistic subjects and one of the controls showed slight levels of measles virus in their sample. The majority of the children had no trace of measles RNA in their bowels, dispelling the idea that the presence of measles RNA caused either the children's autism or their GI disturbances.

The authors noted that children with autism and GI issues were more likely to exhibit regressive tendencies, such as the loss of previously acquired social and language skills, and may represent a distinct autism subtype.

Risk Factors: What Caused This to Happen and Can It Be Prevented?

New research has provided more insight into potential genetic and environmental risk factors for ASD.

By looking at genome-wide scans of people on the autism spectrum and comparing them with typically developing individuals, researchers can identify changes to specific genes that may contribute to ASD. These genetic variants result from deletions and duplications in DNA, many of which have only recently been identified. While specific genetic variants account for only a small percentage of cases, researchers are making headway in understanding the complex genetic underpinnings of the autism spectrum disorders.

Recent research has indicated that several genes involved in the formation and function of synapses are linked to ASD. One particular variant of interest is CNTNAP2 (Contactin associated protein-like 2).[20] [21] Located on chromosome 7, the gene has been found to be enriched in regions of the brain critical for language development and was shown in one study to be related to when boys with autism say their first word.[22] Another study found that a mutated version of a gene called neurexin 1, which is in the same family as CNTNAP2, was present in two subjects with ASD.[23] The father of one of the subjects with the neurexin 1 variant has the same chromosomal abnormality but did not have ASD, showing that other factors must also contribute for the disorder to occur.

Several complete genomic scans have found scores of distinct microdeletions and microduplications – tiny subtractions or additions to the chromosome not apparent using standard microscopic analysis – that are unique to people with autism. These microdeletions and microduplications are also known as copy number variants (CNV) and are believed to cause gene dosage imbalances that can contribute to health conditions and disorders. One study found 51 microdeletions and microduplications that occurred in about 12 percent of the subjects with ASD.[24] Of the 51 CNV, 44 were inherited from a parent, while 7 arose spontaneously. Researchers identified three separate microduplications that were passed from mother to child located in a region on chromosome 15. Another study found 277 variants in 44 percent of the subjects with ASD.[25]

Studies have also focused on a region on chromosome 16 that contains genes involved in both brain development and immune system function.[26] A DNA scan of 1,441 children with ASD showed that five of the children carried microdeletions in chromosome 16, while seven children had microduplications in the same region.[27] In a very small percentage of people in the study, changes to this region of chromosome 16 were also linked to developmental disorders other than autism including attention deficit hyperactivity disorder (ADHD) and schizophrenia.

Abnormalities on other chromosomes have also been implicated in ASD. One study identified microdeletions and microduplications on chromosome 1 that are associated with autism, mental retardation, and congenital anomalies.[28] Overall, these studies suggest that copy number variation may be a common mechanism contributing to the development of autism by causing gene dosage imbalances, and that genes identified through these studies may be worthy of closer examination in future research.

While there seem to be a variety of genes which contribute to the development of autism, researchers found a common biological link between several identified in one study of families with shared ancestry.[29] The study examined 88 families with autistic children where parents were first or second cousins. Nineteen of the families studied had two or more cases of autism. Related parents are more likely to have genetic similarities, so studying them increases the likelihood of finding rare recessive genetic traits that are contributing to the family history of autism.

The researchers were able to identify several genes that may contribute to familial autism, including some that contained large inherited deletions and smaller deletions, as well as some changes in non-coding DNA, which may influence the proper expression and dosage of critical genes. Many of the genes identified are regulated by neuronal activity and mutations in these genes may interfere with the brain's ability to create the synaptic connections that are formed in relation to a child's early experiences. These connections are a critical foundation for further brain development. The authors hypothesize that changes in genes that regulate the formation of these connections may contribute to development of autism.

Other risk factors point strongly to a heritable component to autism. Recent studies showed that the age of a child's mother or father contributes to the risk of autism. Mothers who are 35 years of age or older and fathers 40 years of age or older are significantly more likely to have a child on the autism spectrum.[30] Researchers looked at information about the parents of 1,251 children with autism spectrum disorder and found that having an older mother and/or father was a risk factor for autism. After controlling for other factors, the study found that mothers 35 or older were 30 percent more likely to have a child with ASD than 25- to 29-year-old mothers. Fathers aged 40 or older were 40 percent more likely when compared to fathers 25- to 29-years-old. When both parents were older, their first child was three times as likely to be on the spectrum than a child with two or more older siblings born to younger parents.

A Swedish study also found that people who had been hospitalized for a psychiatric disorder were more likely to have a child with autism than parents of typically developing children.[31] Mothers and fathers diagnosed with schizophrenia were nearly twice as likely to have a child with ASD compared to the general public. Mothers of children with ASD were more likely to have been diagnosed with depression and personality disorders. The same was not true for fathers of autistic children.

Some have also theorized that early umbilical cord clamping may be a risk factor for autism due to possible impact of oxygen deprivation, lower blood volume and other effects.

Researchers recently undertook a review of results from eleven randomized controlled trial studies to determine possible risks and benefits of early versus late cord clamping after birth. While the study did not directly measure the relationship between cord clamping and autism, it did show that children who had their cords clamped after one minute had greater iron levels than those clamped earlier because the extra time prior to clamping allows for transfer of more fetal blood from the placenta to the newborn. Higher levels of iron are associated with better health outcomes, including reduced risk for anemia.[32]

However, infants who had later clamping were also more likely to have jaundice that needed to be treated with phototherapy, caused by the inefficiency of the newborn's liver in processing bilirubin in the blood, which can be exacerbated by the increased blood volume associated with later clamping. Policies on clamping vary – some doctors clamp within a minute after birth while others wait longer or until cord pulsation stops. The study concluded that cord clamping either early or late carries both risks and benefits.

Other birth factors have been linked to autism. Children with the ASD are more likely to be born in certain seasons, according to a new study.[33] After looking at the birth pattern of children with autism, researchers found that April, June, and October were peak months for single births. Peaks occurred 2 to 4 weeks later for multiples with autism. Multiple births of boys with ASD were most frequent in March, May, and September. While the artificial cut-off of months or seasons may hide trends or enhance them, overall this study suggests that non-inherited factors may play a role in the development of autism.

Once a child is born, other factors may predict the likelihood of developing autism. Looking into another person's eyes conveys meaning and is an important part of social interaction. At an early age, typically developing infants show a preference for looking at a person's eyes compared to other parts of the face. [34] Now, new research has found that autistic toddlers show decreased levels of eye contact and increased fixation on mouths by the age of 2 years old, when compared to typically developing children.[35] Additionally, less eye contact predicted greater levels of social disability. These findings could prove useful for diagnosing autism earlier and measuring symptom severity.

Vaccines

Several studies published in 2008 investigated the relationship between thimerosal and the onset of autism. Researchers found that autism rates in California continued to increase even after thimerosal was removed from nearly all childhood vaccines by 2001.[36] If thimerosal was a primary cause of autism, new diagnoses would be expected to decline significantly as exposure decreased. The study examined the rates of autism in children 3 to 12 years old that were reported to the California Department of Developmental Services (CDDS) from January 1995 to March 2007, and instead, found a steady increase in prevalence. Since 2004, the increase in California's autism rates has been greater than that for other developmental disabilities, as a whole.

Dr. Eric Fombonne argues against the involvement of either thimerosal or the MMR vaccine in the development of ASD in his commentary, "Thimerosal Disappears but Autism Remains."[37] He notes that while different investigators have conducted large-scale studies using a variety of designs, the overwhelming majority have failed to show any evidence of a link between autism and immunization. Studies have also failed to find significant evidence of mercury poisoning or the persistence of measles virus in children with autism.[38] Several studies have been conducted that failed to show an increased susceptibility to injury from exposure to mercury or the MMR vaccine in a specific subgroup of autistic children. Fombonne cited the CDDS study described above, as well as studies conducted in Canada and Denmark, which describe a continued rise in rates of ASD diagnoses, even after the removal of thimerosal from childhood vaccines.

However, one 2008 study did purport to find evidence of an association between thimerosal and neurodevelopmental disorders in children.[39] At 28 weeks of pregnancy, Rhesus factor (Rh)- negative mothers who are carrying Rh-positive children are given a preparation of immune globulins in order to prevent a potentially dangerous immune response in both the mother and child at the time of delivery. Until its removal in 2002, the immune globulin injection contained the mercury-based preservative thimerosal. The researchers hypothesized that if prenatal exposure to the immune globulin was a risk factor for neurodevelopmental disorders, more mothers of children with these disorders would be Rh-negative when compared to a control group. After examining 298 children with a range of neurodevelopmental disorders, the study found that children with ASD born before 2002 were significantly more likely to have Rh-negative mothers than the control population. They found no difference in the prevalence of Rh-negative mothers after 2002, leading the authors to conclude that thimerosal contributed to the children's risk for developing neurodevelopmental disorders.

Treatment: Which Treatments and Interventions Will Help?

In 2008, progress was made in several different types of treatments and interventions for ASD, four of which are described in this section.

Recently, scientists discovered that the drug rapamycin, an immunosuppressant drug normally used to prevent organ rejection after transplant, reduces neurological symptoms in mice with tuberous sclerosis complex (TSC),[40] a rare genetic disorder that often co-occurs with mental retardation, epilepsy, and autism. Researchers were able to reverse learning and memory deficits in mice carrying the genetic mutation which causes TSC by injecting rapamycin. The results suggest that cognitive deficits resulting from TSC are caused by reversible changes in brain function rather than permanent damage to the developing brain. These findings could be the first step in discovering effective drug therapies for autism and related developmental disorders. Currently, there are few pharmacologic treatment options for people with ASD.

Another study investigating ASD interventions found that computerized training has shown promise in helping people with autism process facial expressions.[41] Many people with ASD have trouble recognizing and remembering faces because they process the information differently than typically developing people.[42] They often focus on the outer portions of the face instead of the more important central features such as the eyes and nose.[43] Typically developing people are able to recognize faces by processing the face as a whole and paying attention to the specific configuration between features.[44]

The 2008 study suggests that facial processing can be improved through training. Five high-functioning autistic men were shown black and white photos of faces on a computer screen and given specific instructions about how their eyes should navigate the pictures. They then practiced matching similar faces and classifying faces into categories such as "young" and "old." Subjects were told to pay attention to the central facial features and were given tasks where only cropped portions of the faces were visible.

After their training, the subjects showed more sensitivity to facial configuration than five men with ASD who had not been trained. However, the training did not improve the men's ability to process the face as a whole; rather they continued to focus on individual features.

In 2008 intervention studies, two different play interventions showed the ability to improve language development in preschool children with autism.[45] Three- and four-year-old children with autism worked with an instructor to improve either their joint attention (the ability to share in a common experience with another person; i.e., 'Look at the big dog!') or their symbolic play (the ability to create pretend roles and imagined scene; i.e., 'You're going to play the mom'). The children attended the same day treatment program but had varying levels of developmental abilities.

After receiving the play interventions for 30 minutes a day for five to six weeks, both the joint attention and the symbolic play groups showed greater degrees of expressive language 12 months later when compared to a control group. Children who had previously exhibited the lowest language abilities, showed greatest gains from the joint play intervention. These findings suggest that honing joint attention and symbolic play skills can lead to improved language skills.

Finally, another intervention study provided insight into how low-functioning children with autism learn to associate pictures, words and real-world objects. Forms of augmentative and alternative communication such as the Picture Exchange Communication System (PECS) use pictures to represent real actions and objects. However, research shows that children with autism may not be able to comprehend the symbolic nature of pictures,[46] a concept that typically-developing children generally demonstrate by two years of age.

Twenty-two children with autism were taught a new word, such as "whisk," and trained to pair it with a novel picture of a whisk. Half the children in the study were PECS-users, while the other half were not. The children were then shown an actual whisk (having never seen one before) alongside a picture of the whisk and asked to indicate which one was the whisk. The majority of the children with autism associated the word with the picture rather than the object, unlike their typically developing peers with similar receptive language skills. The researchers confirmed that these results were not due to the children's preference for selecting pictures, or their tendency to perseverate on a previous correct response. Autistic children who used PECS were much more likely to point to the picture than non-PECS users.

These results indicate that children with autism are learning picture-word and word-object pairings through association rather than grasping the symbolic nature of pictures. Children who were non-verbal and/or who were

PECS users were particularly likely to associate a word with the picture rather than the real object.

Services and Supports: Which Treatments and Interventions Will Help?

Major scientific advances were made during 2008 in three areas related to services and supports for people with autism. Recent studies investigated the influence of information sources on school children's attitudes towards autism, medical costs for children and adolescents with ASD, and the effects of ASD on household income.

Children with autism benefit in many ways by being included in a classroom with their typically developing peers. However, when entering the mainstream classroom, children with ASD may face negative attitudes from other children. A study published in 2008 may have implications for shaping school-aged children's attitudes about autism.[47] The study reports that children's attitudes about a new classmate with autism are affected based on who provides information about the disorder.

A group of 296 children in third, fourth, and fifth grade were given information about an unfamiliar autistic student by their teacher, a video, or an actor portraying the new child's mother, father, or physician. The children were given information about autism by the different sources, then shown a short videotaped clip of a 12-year-old male actor who is identified as "Robby." In the video, Robby displays typically autistic behavior by rocking his body, making stereotypic hand movements, and averting his gaze. A narrator describes the similarities between Robby and the children viewing the video.

The study showed that certain age groups responded more favorably to different sources by measuring the children's cognitive and behavioral attitudes toward Robby after receiving information about autism from the various sources. Cognitive attitudes are beliefs that the child holds about people with autism while behavioral attitudes reflect how the child intends to interact with the person. Fifth-graders showed more favorable cognitive and behavioral attitudes toward Robby when receiving information about autism from a teacher or doctor rather than the child's parent, whereas the third-graders' attitudes were more influenced by Robby's mother.

These findings suggest that when introducing children on the autism spectrum into mainstream classrooms, the entire class would benefit from receiving education about ASD from multiple sources.

Another 2008 study confirmed what parents of children with ASD already knew -- medical expenses related to care of individuals with ASD are costly. A national study of 1.2 million privately-insured children with an ASD diagnosis found that children and adolescents with ASD incur medical expenses that average $3,110 to $6,200 greater per year than for typically developing children.[48] This represents an average cost increase of 4.1 to 6.2 percent. The difference in medical costs was greatest for children with ASD from one to four years of age.

Medical costs were calculated using the total amount of reimbursements or out-of-pocket expenses incurred, though did not include the cost of complementary and alternative therapies, which are rarely covered by insurance.

The findings of this study build on previous studies that have illustrated the heavy burden of medical costs associated with ASD. In 2007, another study calculated that during the first five years of life, a child with ASD will average $35,000 in direct medical costs per year.[49] These costs begin to decline when the child reaches eight years of age, to approximately $6,000 annually, and continue to decline over the lifespan.

Adding to the financial strain, families with children on the spectrum have been shown to lose a significant portion of household income -- sometimes as a result of one parent leaving the workforce to care for his or her child. One study found that a family with an autistic child lost an average of $6200 or 14 percent of their yearly income.[50] This, combined with the additional out-of-pocket medical expenses, represents a significant burden for families of children with ASD. The study surveyed parents of 11,684 children who were currently in kindergarten to eighth grade and identified 131 children who had been diagnosed with ASD. Researchers then compared reported household income for families of children with ASD to families of similar demographic and educational characteristics with typically developing children. Families of children with ASD were significantly less likely to live in a higher income household after controlling for the parent's level of education, type of family, location, and other variables. These families also reported incomes that averaged $6,200 less than other similar families without an autistic child.

Outcomes: What Does the Future Hold?

In 2008, there were a number of important advances in understanding what the future holds for people with ASD.

In one study, researchers reviewed outcome studies of children who had reportedly "recovered" from autism, meaning they had initially been diagnosed with the disorder but now showed a normal trajectory of development. Some researchers and clinicians are skeptical that "recovery" from autism can occur. However, the study authors evaluated evidence that between 3 and 25 percent of children lose their ASD diagnosis.[51]

Certain factors may contribute to whether a child will lose their ASD diagnosis. After analyzing the results of other recovery studies, the review found that relatively high intelligence, verbal and motor imitation and receptive language predicted which children had lost their diagnosis. Children diagnosed with Pervasive Developmental Disorder-Not Otherwise Specified (PDDNOS) were more likely to report recovery, as were those who had been diagnosed and treated for autism at an earlier age. Overall symptom severity did not predict which children would lose their ASD diagnosis, nor did measures of head growth. Children with seizures, mental retardation and genetic disorders were less likely to report recovery. Losing the ASD diagnosis did not mean that children were problem-free. Many children reportedly had remaining problems such as tics, depression, phobias, and ADHD.

What brings about recovery? The review suggested several hypotheses about possible mechanisms for future research, including the idea that early interventions provide enriched environments for the children to overcome their symptoms or that the extreme repetition of intensive early interventions lead to some sort of neural reorganization. Other potential factors that may have contributed to recovery include reinforcing the value of social stimuli, repeatedly practicing weak skills, and reducing stress. While there is no evidence that biomedical interventions alone will result in recovery from autism, the authors conclude that good nutrition and sleep quality is beneficial to all children with ASD.

Two important studies in 2008 investigated the early predictors of later language development. One study found that two types of motor skills, oral and manual, could be used to predict speech fluency later in life.[52] Speaking requires the complex coordination of oral-motor skills such as pursing the lips and thrusting the tongue. Oral-motor skills are also closely tied with manual-motor skills (i.e., hand and finger movements) in typically developing children.

Parents of children with autism were interviewed about their child's early development, and were asked to recall specifics about their child's oral-motor and manual motors at key developmental milestones. (i.e., Did he stick out his tongue on request at 24 months? Did he grab glasses off your face at six months?)

Early home videos were used to corroborate parental accounts. Researchers than assessed the current language skills of 115 autistic children, who were about 8 years old on average at the time. The study found that infant and toddler oral- and manual-motor skills could predict level of speech fluency for children around eight years of age to early teens. The study also showed that early motor skills differed significantly between autistic and typically developing children.

Another language development study found that certain behaviors can predict which children will show the most language growth.[53] Autistic children who respond to others' attempts to share in observing an object or event (for example, playing with the same toy or pointing out an interesting happening) show more language growth than those who do not respond to bids for joint attention.

In a study of 28 children with ASD, those who were able to coordinate their interest in external events or objects had significantly greater language gains three to four years later. During play, the parents' responsiveness to their child's focus of attention and ongoing activity also predicted future language development.

Interestingly, these gains were independent of the child's IQ, mental age, or initial language skills.

A long-term study of 341 Danish citizens with ASD found that the mortality rate for the participants was nearly double that of the typically developing population when matched for age and gender. [54] In total, 26 of the 341 people with ASD died during the study period from 1960- 2006; nearly double the 13.5 deaths that would have been expected. Mortality risk was greatest during the first fifteen years post-diagnosis, and was not affected by IQ levels.

Epilepsy and infectious diseases such as meningitis, pneumonia, and appendicitis were common causes of death for people with ASD. The high mortality from epilepsy and related issues suggests that the disorder may pose an even greater risk for people with ASD than for typically- developing individuals with epilepsy. The study also found that people with ASD may be more prone to fatal accidents.

The study authors suggest that direct care staff receive training to better manage potentially life-threatening physical illnesses that commonly affect people with ASD and that additional focus on accident risks and prevention would be beneficial.

Articles Selected for 2008 Summary of Advances

Journal Article	Funding Information	Journal Impact Factor (2008)*
Alarcón, M., B. S. Abrahams, et al. (2008). "Linkage, Association, and Gene-Expression Analyses Identify CNTNAP2 as an Autism-Susceptibility Gene." Am. J. Hum. Genet. 82(1): 150- 159.	National Institute of Mental Health (NIMH) grant R01 MH64547, R01 MH076431, a NARSAD Young Investigator award, a MIND Institute Fellowship, an NRSA from NINDS, a Tourette Syndrome Association Fellowship, the UCLA Center for Autism Research and Treatment, the Cure Autism Now foundation, The Simons Foundation, and co-funding from the National Alliance for Autism Research and the Southwestern Autism Research and Resource Center	10.153
Arking, D. E., D. J. Cutler, et al. (2008). "A common genetic variant in the neurexin superfamily member CNTNAP2 increases familial risk of autism." Am. J. Hum. Genet. 82(1): 160- 4. Epub 2008/01/09.	National Institutes of Health (NIH) grants MH52708, MH39437, MH00219, and MH00980; National Health Medical Research Council grant 0034328; and by grants from the Scottish Rite, the Spunk Fund, Inc., the Rebecca and Solomon Baker Fund, the APEX Foundation, the National Alliance for Research in Schizophrenia and Affective Disorders (NARSAD), the endowment fund of the Nancy Pritzker Laboratory (Stanford); and the Autism Society of America, and the Janet M. Grace Pervasive Developmental Disorders Fund	10.153
Bailey, A. R., B. N. Giunta, et al. (2008). "Peripheral biomarkers in Autism: secreted amyloid precursor protein-alpha as a probable key player in early diagnosis." Int J Clin Exp Med 1(4): 338- 44. Epub 2008/12/17.	Robert A. Silver foundation and a grant for the NIH/NIMH	N/A
Bakkaloglu, B., B. J. O'Roak, et al.	NIH grant K23 RR16118-04, the	10.153

Journal Article	Funding Information	Journal Impact Factor (2008)*
(2008). "Molecular Cytogenetic Analysis and Resequencing of Contactin Associated Protein-Like 2 in Autism Spectrum Disorders." Am. J. Hum. Genet. 82(1): 165-173.	Lawrence Family, the Shephard Foundation, National Institute on Drug Abuse (NIDA) grant R01 DA018928, NIMH grant R01 MH 64547, the UCLA Center for Autism Research and Treatment, and the Cure Autism Now Foundation	
Braunschweig, D., P. Ashwood, et al. (2008). "Autism: maternally derived antibodies specific for fetal brain proteins." Neurotoxicology 29(2): 226- 31. Epub 2007/12/15.	National Institute of Environmental Health Sciences (NIEHS), 1 P01 ES11269-01, the U.S. Environmental Protection Agency (U.S. EPA) through the Science to Achieve Results (STAR) program (Grant R829388), and the UC Davis M.I.N.D. Institute	2.409
Chahrour, M., S. Y. Jung, et al. (2008). "MeCP2, a key contributor to neurological disease, activates and represses transcription." Science 320(5880): 1224-9. Epub 2008/05/31.	NIH/National Institute of Neurological Disorders and Stroke (NINDS) grant NS057819, National Institute of Child Health and Human Development (NICHD) Mental Retardation and Developmental Disabilities Research Center HD024064, the International Rett Syndrome Foundation, the Simons Foundation, and a Howard Hughes Medical Institute investigator award	28.103
Chiu, P. H., M. A. Kayali, et al. (2008). "Self responses along cingulate cortex reveal quantitative neural phenotype for high-functioning autism." Neuron 57(3): 463-73. Epub 2008/02/08.	The Kane Family Foundation, The Dana Foundation and Autism Speaks, National Institute on Drug Abuse (NIDA) (R01 DA11723), National Institute of Neurological Disorders and Stroke (NINDS) (R01 NS045790), The Angel Williamson Imaging Center, and the American Psychological Association (T32 MH18882)	14.170
Choi, Y. J., A. Di Nardo, et al. (2008). "Tuberous sclerosis complex proteins control axon formation." Genes Dev. 22(18): 2485-95. Epub 2008/09/17.	Hearst Fund, the Tuberous Sclerosis Alliance, Manton Foundation, and a grant from Children's Hospital Boston Mental Retardation and Developmental Disability Research Center (P01HD18655), NIH grant	13.623

Journal Article	Funding Information	Journal Impact Factor (2008)*
	NS031535 and NS058956, an American Academy of Neurology/SMA Young Investigator award and a Leukemia and Lymphoma Society Scholar award	
Christian, S. L., C. W. Brune, et al. (2008). "Novel submicroscopic chromosomal abnormalities detected in autism spectrum disorder." Biol. Psychiatry 63(12): 1111-7. Epub 2008/04/01.	National Alliance for Autism Research and the National Institute of Neurological Diseases and Stroke (NINDS) (R01 NS51812), the National Institutes of Health/National Cancer Institute (NCI), (P30 CA016056) (RPCI Cancer Center Support Grant).	8.672
Daniels, J.L., U. Forssen, et al. (2008). Parental psychiatric disorders associated with autism spectrum disorders in the offspring [erratum appears in Pediatrics 2008 Nov;122(5):1162] Pediatrics 121(5):e1357-62.	Centers for Disease Control and Prevention (CDC)	4.789
Durkin, M. S., M. J. Maenner, et al. (2008). "Advanced parental age and the risk of autism spectrum disorder." Am. J. Epidemiol. 168(11): 1268-76. Epub 2008/10/24.	Centers for Disease Control and Prevention (CDC), Cooperative Agreements UR3/CCU523235 and UR3/DD000078 and the University of Wisconsin	5.454
Ehninger, D., S. Han, et al. (2008). "Reversal of learning deficits in a Tsc2+/- mouse model of tuberous sclerosis." Nat. Med. 14(8): 843-8. Epub 2008/06/24.	Deutsche Forschungsgemeinschaft EH223/2-1, National Institutes of Health R01-NS38480, National Institutes of Health NS24279, and Autism Speaks	27.553
Faja, S., E. Aylward, et al. (2008). "Becoming a face expert: a computerized face-training program for high- functioning individuals with autism spectrum disorders." Developmental neuropsychology 33(1): 1-24.	National Institute of Child Health and Human Development (NICHD) (U19HD34565, P50HD066782), the National Institute of Mental Health (NIMH) (U54MH066399), and the Cure Autism Now Foundation	1.964
Fombonne, E. (2008). "Thimerosal disappears but autism remains." Arch. Gen. Psychiatry 65(1): 15-16.	N/A	14.273
Geier, D. A., E. Mumper, et al. (2008). "Neurodevelopmental	N/A	1.359

Journal Article	Funding Information	Journal Impact Factor (2008)*
disorders, maternal Rh-negativity, and Rho(D) immune globulins: a multi-center assessment." Neuro Endocrinology Letters 29(2): 272-80.		
Gernsbacher, M.A., E.A. Sauer, et al. (2008). "Infant and toddler oral- and manual-motor skills predict later speech fluency in autism." J. Child Psychol. Psychiatry. 49(1):43-50. Epub 2007/11/01.	National Alliance for Autism Research and the National Institute of Deafness and Communication Disorder (NIDCD) (DC 5365)	4.854
Gregg, J. P., L. Lit, et al. (2008). "Gene expression changes in children with autism." Genomics 91(1): 22-9. Epub 2007/11/17.	NIEHS 1 P01 ES11269-01 and U.S. Environmental Protection Agency R829388, the University of California at Davis MIND Institute, and NINDS NS028167 and NS043252	3.075
Helt, M., E. Kelley, et al. (2008). "Can children with autism recover? If so, how?" Neuropsychol. Rev. 18(4): 339-66. Epub 2008/11/15.	N/A	3.349
Hornig, M., T. Briese, et al. (2008). "Lack of Association between Measles Virus Vaccine and Autism with Enteropathy: A Case- Control Study." PLoS ONE 3(9): e3140.	CDC grant U50 CCU522351 to AAP and by National Institutes of Health awards AI57158 (Northeast Biodefense Center-Lipkin), HL083850, and NS47537	N/A
Jones, W., K. Carr, et al. (2008). "Absence of preferential looking to the eyes of approaching adults predicts level of social disability in 2-year-old toddlers with autism spectrum disorder." Arch. Gen. Psychiatry 65(8): 946-54. Epub 2008/08/06.	National Institutes of Mental Health grant U54- MH66494, Autism Speaks, the Simons Foundation, and the American Psychological Foundation Elizabeth Munsterberg Koppitz Award	14.273
Kasari, C., T. Paparella, et al. (2008). "Language outcome in autism: randomized comparison of joint attention and play interventions." J. Consult. Clin. Psychol. 76(1): 125-37.	National Institutes of Child Health and Development (NICHD) grant (HD035470), the Collaborative Programs of Excellence in Autism Network, and the Department of Child Psychiatry at the University of California, Los Angeles	4.991
Kim, H. G., S. Kishikawa, et al. (2008). "Disruption of Neurexin 1	National Institutes of Health grants P01-GM061354, U19- HD35482,	10.153

Journal Article	Funding Information	Journal Impact Factor (2008)*
Associated with Autism Spectrum Disorder." Am. J. Hum. Genet. 82(1): 199-207.	P01-HD00300838, and R01-NS16648, a NARSAD Distinguished Investigator Award, and a Young Investigator Award from the Children's Tumor Foundation	
Kumar, R. A., S. KaraMohamed, et al. (2008). "Recurrent 16p11.2 microdeletions in autism." Hum. Mol. Genet. 17(4): 628- 38. Epub 2007/12/25.	National Institutes of Health, National Institute of Neurological Diseases and Stroke (1R01NS51812) and National Institute of Mental Health (1R01MH64547-01), the National Alliance for Autism Research, and an Autism Speaks Post-Doctoral Fellowship Award, and a grant from the National Institute of Mental Health (NIMH) (MH64547)	7.249
Lee, L. C., C. J. Newschaffer, et al. (2008). "Variation in season of birth in singleton and multiple births concordant for autism spectrum disorders." Paediatr. Perinat. Epidemiol. 22(2): 172-9. Epub 2008/02/27.	Centers for Disease Control and Prevention (CDC) cooperative agreement U10/CCU320408-05, and Cure Autism Now (CAN)	1.660
Marshall, C. R., A. Noor, et al. (2008). "Structural variation of chromosomes in autism spectrum disorder." Am. J. Hum. Genet. 82(2): 477-88. Epub 2008/02/07.	Genome Canada/Ontario Genomics Institute, the Canadian Institutes of Health Research (CIHR), the McLaughlin Centre for Molecular Medicine, the Canadian Institute of Advanced Research, Autism Speaks, the McMaster Children's Hospital Foundation, the Hospital for Sick Children (SickKids) Foundation, the German National Genome Research Network (NGFN), the National Alliance for Research on Schizophrenia and Depression (NARSAD), the Netherlands Organization for Scientific Research and the Royal Netherlands Academy of Arts and Sciences, a Health Scholar award from the Alberta Heritage	10.153

Journal Article	Funding Information	Journal Impact Factor (2008)*
	Foundation for Medical Research and a CIHR New Investigator award	
McDonald, S. J., P. Middleton (2008) Effect of timing of umbilical cord clamping of term infants on maternal and neonatal outcomes. Cochrane Database of Systematic Reviews, 10.1002/14651858.CD004074.pub2	N/A	5.182
Mefford, H. C., A. J. Sharp, et al. (2008). "Recurrent rearrangements of chromosome 1q21.1 and variable pediatric phenotypes." N. Engl. J. Med. 359(16): 1685-99. Epub 2008/09/12.	National Institutes of Health (HD043569), the South Carolina Department of Disabilities and Special Needs, the Wellcome Trust (061183), the André & Cyprien Foundation and the University Hospitals of Geneva, and the European Union (project 219250) AnEUploidy project (037627), the Health Research Board, the Dutch Foundation for Brain Research (Hersenstichting grant 2008(1) 34), the Oxford Partnership Comprehensive Biomedical Research Centre, the Cambridge Biomedical Research Centre, with funding from the United Kingdom Department of Health's National Institute for Health Research Biomedical Research Centres funding scheme, the National Genetics Reference Laboratory (Wessex) by the United Kingdom Department of Health, the Research Foundation–Flanders, and the Howard Hughes Medical Institute	50.017
Montes, G., J.S. Halterman (2008). "Association of Childhood Autism Spectrum Disorders and Loss of Family Income." Pediatrics 2008; 121;e821-e826.	N/A	4.789
Morrow, E. M., S. Y. Yoo, et al. (2008). "Identifying autism loci and genes by tracing recent shared	Cure Autism Now (CAN), the Nancy Lurie Marks Family Foundation, the Simons Foundation,	28.103

Journal Article	Funding Information	Journal Impact Factor (2008)*
ancestry." Science 321(5886): 218-23. Epub 2008/07/16.	the Harvard Kuwait Project, the Developmental Disabilities Research Center of Children's Hospital Boston (5P30HD018655-26), the Clinical Investigator Training Program of Harvard and Massachusetts Institute of Technology in collaboration with Pfizer Inc. and Merck & Co., the Anne and Paul Marcus Foundation, the Charles H. Hood Foundation, and NIH (1K23MH080954-01, 1R01 MH083565, 1K01MH71801, and 5R01NS048276-05	
Morton, J. F. and J. M. Campbell (2008). "Information source affects peers' initial attitudes toward autism." Res. Dev. Disabil. 29(3): 189-201. Epub 2007 Mar 27.	N/A	4.475
Mouridsen, S. E., H. Bronnum-Hansen, et al. (2008). "Mortality and causes of death in autism spectrum disorders: an update." Autism 12(4): 403-14. Epub 2008/06/27.	N/A	1.937
Pinto-Martin, J.A., L.M. Young, et al. (2008). Screening strategies for autism spectrum disorders in pediatric primary care. Journal of Developmental and Behavioral Pediatrics, 29(5), 1-6.	Centers for Disease Control and Prevention (CDC)	2.487
Preissler, M. A. (2008). "Associative learning of pictures and words by low-functioning children with autism." Autism: the international journal of research and practice 12(3): 231-48.	N/A	1.937
Schechter, R., J. K. Grether (2008). "Continuing increases in autism reported to California's developmental services system: mercury in retrograde." Arch. Gen. Psychiatry 65(1): 19-24. Epub 2008/01/09.	California Department of Public Health	14.273

Journal Article	Funding Information	Journal Impact Factor (2008)*
Shimabukuro, T.T., S. D. Grosse, et al. (2008). "Medical Expenditures for Children with an Autism Spectrum Disorder in a Privately Insured Population". J Autism Dev Disord (2008) 38:546–552.	Centers for Disease Control and Prevention (CDC)	3.348
Siller, M., M. Sigman (2008). "Modeling longitudinal change in the language abilities of children with autism: parent behaviors and child characteristics as predictors of change." Dev. Psychol. 44(6):1691-704.	N/A	3.425
Weiss, L. A., V. Shen, et al. (2008). "Association between microdeletion and microduplication at 16p11.2 and autism." N. Engl. J. Med. 358(7): 667-75. Epub 2008/01/11.	Autism Consortium, a Ruth L. Kirschstein National Research Service Award, a Sidney Sax fellowship from the National Health and Medical Research Council of Australia, a grant from the Ellison Foundation, the Simons Foundation, and a grant (R01-MN071425-01A1) from the National Institute of Mental Health	50.017

* Journal impact factor is a measure of the number of citations an indexed journal receives annually and may be used to rank the relative importance of the journal. Higher impact factor scores represent a greater number of citations.

End Notes

[1] Interagency Autism Coordinating Committee. (2009). *The Interagency Autism Coordinating Committee Strategic Plan for Autism Spectrum Disorder Research.* Retrieved 06-25-09 from http://www.iacc.hhs.gov/reports/2009/iacc-strategic-plan-forautism-spectrum-disorder - research-jan26.shtml

[2] Eaves, L.C., Ho, H.H. (2004). The very early identification of autism: outcome to age 4 1/2 - 5. *J Autism Dev Disord* 34:367-378.

[3] Filipek, P.A., Accardo, P.J. Ashwal, S., et al. (2000) Practice parameter: screening and diagnosis of autism: Report of the Quality Standards Subcommittee of the American Academy of Neurology and Child Neurology Society. *Neurology* 55:468-479.

[4] Lord, C., McGee, J. (2001). *Educating Children with Autism.* Washington DC: National Academy Press.

[5] Mandell, D.S., Novak, M.M., Zubritsky, C.D. (2005). Factors associated with age of diagnosis among children with autism spectrum disorders. *Pediatrics* 116:1480-1486.

[6] Howlin, P. Asgharian, A. (1999). The diagnosis of autism and Asperger syndrome: findings from a survey of 770 families. *Dev Child Neurol* 41:834-839.

[7] **Chiu, P. H., Kayali, M.A., et al. (2008). "Self responses along cingulate cortex reveal quantitative neural phenotype for high-functioning autism."** ***Neuron*** **57(3): 463-73. Epub 2008/02/08. (*Articles in bold were selected by the IACC for the 2008 Summary of Advances)**

[8] **Pinto-Martin, J.A., Young, L.M., et al. (2008). Screening strategies for autism spectrum disorders in pediatric primary care.** ***Journal of Developmental and Behavioral Pediatrics*** **29(5): 1-6.**

[9] Glascoe, F.P. (2003). Parents' evaluation of developmental status: how well do parents' concerns identify children with behavioral and emotional problems. *Clin Pediatr (Phila)* 42:133–138.

[10] Robins, D.L., Fein, D., et al. (2001). The Modified Checklist for Autism in Toddlers: an initial study investigating the early detection of autism and pervasive developmental disorders. *J Autism Dev Disord* 31:131–144

[11] American Academy of Pediatrics. (2006). Identifying infants and young children with developmental disorders in the Medical Home: an algorithm for developmental surveillance and screening. *Pediatrics* 118:405–420.

[12] Amir, R.E., Van den Veyver, I.B., et al. (1999). Rett syndrome is caused by mutations in X-linked MECP2, encoding methylCpG-binding protein 2. *Nat Genetics* 23:185.

[13] **Chahrour, M., Jung, S.Y., et al. (2008). "MeCP2, a key contributor to neurological disease, activates and represses transcription."** ***Science*** **320(5880): 1224-9. Epub 2008/05/31.**

[14] **Choi, Y. J., Di Nardo, A., et al. (2008). "Tuberous sclerosis complex proteins control axon formation."** ***Genes Dev*** **22(18): 2485-95. Epub 2008/09/17.**

[15] **Gregg, J. P., Lit, L., et al. (2008). "Gene expression changes in children with autism."** ***Genomics*** **91(1): 22-9. Epub 2007/11/17.**

[16] **Bailey, A. R., Giunta, B.N., et al. (2008). "Peripheral biomarkers in Autism: secreted amyloid precursor protein-alpha as a probable key player in early diagnosis."** ***Int J Clin Exp Med*** **1(4): 338-44. Epub 2008/12/17.**

[17] **Braunschweig, D., Ashwood, P., et al. (2008). "Autism: maternally derived antibodies specific for fetal brain proteins."** ***Neurotoxicology*** **29(2): 226-31. Epub 2007/12/15.**

[18] **Hornig, M., Briese, T., et al. (2008). "Lack of Association between Measles Virus Vaccine and Autism with Enteropathy: A Case-Control Study."** ***PLoS ONE*** **3(9): e3140.**

[19] Wakefield, A.J., Murch, S.H., et al. (1998) Ileal-lymphoid-nodular hyperplasia, non-specific colitis, and pervasive developmental disorder in children. *Lancet* 351: 637–641.

[20] **Arking, D. E., Cutler, D.J., et al. (2008). "A common genetic variant in the neurexin superfamily member CNTNAP2 increases familial risk of autism."** ***Am J Hum Genet*** **82(1): 160-4. Epub 2008/01/09.**

[21] **Bakkaloglu, B., O'Roak, B.J., et al. (2008). "Molecular Cytogenetic Analysis and Resequencing of Contactin Associated Protein-Like 2 in Autism Spectrum Disorders."** ***Am J Hum Genet*** **82(1): 165-173.**

[22] **Alarcón, M., Abrahams, B.S., et al. (2008). "Linkage, Association, and Gene-Expression Analyses Identify CNTNAP2 as an Autism-Susceptibility Gene."** ***Am J Hum Genet*** **82(1): 150-159.**

[23] **Kim, H. G., Kishikawa, S., et al. (2008). "Disruption of Neurexin 1 Associated with Autism Spectrum Disorder."** ***Am J Hum Genet*** **82(1): 199-207.**

[24] **Christian, S. L., Brune, C.W., et al. (2008). "Novel submicroscopic chromosomal abnormalities detected in autism spectrum disorder." *Biol Psychiatry* 63(12): 1111-7. Epub 2008/04/01.**

[25] **Marshall, C. R., Noor, A., et al. (2008). "Structural variation of chromosomes in autism spectrum disorder." *Am J Hum Genet* 82(2): 477-88. Epub 2008/02/07.**

[26] **Kumar, R.A., KaraMohamed, S., et al. (2008). "Recurrent 16p11.2 microdeletions in autism." *Hum Mol Genet* 17(4): 628-38. Epub 2007/12/25.**

[27] **Weiss, L. A., Shen, Y., et al. (2008). "Association between microdeletion and microduplication at 16p11.2 and autism." *N Engl J Med* 358(7): 667-75. Epub 2008/01/11.**

[28] **Mefford, H. C., Sharp, A.J., et al. (2008). "Recurrent rearrangements of chromosome 1q21.1 and variable pediatric phenotypes." *N Engl J Med* 359(16): 1685-99. Epub 2008/09/12.**

[29] **Morrow, E. M., Yoo, S.Y., et al. (2008). "Identifying autism loci and genes by tracing recent shared ancestry." *Science* 321(5886): 218-23. Epub 2008/07/16. *Epidemiol* 168(11): 1268-76. Epub 2008/10/24.**

[30] **Durkin, M. S., Maenner, M.J., et al. (2008). "Advanced parental age and the risk of autism spectrum disorder." Am J *Epidemiol* 168(11): 1268-76. Epub 2008/10/24.**

[31] **Daniels, J.L., Forssen, U., et al. (2008). Parental psychiatric disorders associated with autism spectrum disorders in the offspring. [erratum appears in Pediatrics. 2008 Nov;122(5):1162.]. *Pediatrics* 121(5):e1357-62.**

[32] **McDonald, S. J., Middleton, P. (2008) Effect of timing of umbilical cord clamping of term infants on maternal and neonatal outcomes. *Cochrane Database of Systematic Reviews* 10.1002/14651858.CD004074.pub2**

[33] **Lee, L. C., Newschaffer, C.J., et al. (2008). "Variation in season of birth in singleton and multiple births concordant for autism spectrum disorders." *Paediatr Perinat Epidemiol* 22(2): 172-9. Epub 2008/02/27.**

[34] Haith, M.M., Bergman, T., et al. (1977). Eye contact and face scanning in early infancy. *Science* 198(4319):853-855.

[35] **Jones, W., Carr, K., et al. (2008). "Absence of preferential looking to the eyes of approaching adults predicts level of social disability in 2-year-old toddlers with autism spectrum disorder." *Arch Gen Psychiatry* 65(8): 946-54. Epub 2008/08/06.**

[36] **Schechter, R., Grether, J.K. (2008). "Continuing increases in autism reported to California's developmental services system: mercury in retrograde." *Arch Gen Psychiatry* 65(1): 19-24. Epub 2008/01/09.**

[37] **Fombonne, E. (2008). "Thimerosal disappears but autism remains." *Arch Gen Psychiatry* 65(1): 15-16.**

[38] **Hornig, M., Briese, T., et al. (2008). "Lack of Association between Measles Virus Vaccine and Autism with Enteropathy: A Case-Control Study." *PLoS ONE* 3(9): e3140.**

[39] **Geier, D. A., Mumper, E., et al. (2008). "Neurodevelopmental disorders, maternal Rh-negativity, and Rho(D) immune globulins: a multi-center assessment." *Neuro Endocrinology Letters* 29(2): 272-80.**

[40] **Ehninger, D., Han, S., et al. (2008). "Reversal of learning deficits in a Tsc2+/- mouse model of tuberous sclerosis." *Nat Med* 14(8): 843-8. Epub 2008/06/24.**

[41] **Faja, S., Aylward, E., et al. (2008). "Becoming a face expert: a computerized face-training program for high-functioning individuals with autism spectrum disorders." *Developmental neuropsychology* 33(1): 1-24.**

[42] Davies, S., Bishop, D., et al. (1994) Face perception in children with autism and Asperger's syndrome. *Journal of Child Psychology and Psychiatry* 35: 1033-1057.

[43] Klin, A., Jones, W., et al. (2002). Visual fixation patterns during viewing of naturalistic social situations as predictors of social competence in individuals with autism. *Archives of General Psychiatry* 59: 809-816.

[44] Campbell, R., Coleman, M., et al. (1999) When does the inner-face advantage in familiar face recognition arise and why? *Visual Cognition* 6:197-216.

[45] **Kasari, C., Paparella, T., et al. (2008). "Language outcome in autism: randomized comparison of joint attention and play interventions." *J Consult Clin Psychol* 76(1): 125-37.**

[46] **Preissler, M. A. (2008). "Associative learning of pictures and words by low-functioning children with autism." *Autism: the international journal of research and practice* 12(3): 231-48.**

[47] **Morton, J. F., Campbell, J.M. (2008). "Information source affects peers' initial attitudes toward autism." *Res Dev Disabil* 29(3): 189-201. Epub 2007 Mar 27.**

[48] **Shimabukuro, T.T., Grosse, S.D., et al. (2008). "Medical Expenditures for Children with an Autism Spectrum Disorder in a Privately Insured Population." *J Autism Dev Disord* 38:546–552.**

[49] Ganz, M.L. (2007). The lifetime distribution of the incremental societal costs of autism. *Arch Pediatr Adolesc* Med 161(4):343- 9.

[50] **Montes, G., Halterman, J.S. (2008). "Association of Childhood Autism Spectrum Disorders and Loss of Family Income." *Pediatrics* 2008; 121;e821-e826.**

[51] **Helt, M., Kelley, E., et al. (2008). "Can children with autism recover? If so, how?" *Neuropsychol Rev* 18(4): 339-66. Epub 2008/11/15.**

[52] **Gernsbacher, M.A., Sauer, E.A., et al. (2008). "Infant and toddler oral- and manual-motor skills predict later speech fluency in autism." *J Child Psychol Psychiatry* 49(1):43-50. Epub 2007/11/01.**

[53] **Siller, M., Sigman, M. (2008). "Modeling longitudinal change in the language abilities of children with autism: parent behaviors and child characteristics as predictors of change." *Dev Psychol* 44(6):1691-704.**

[54] **Mouridsen, S. E., Bronnum-Hansen, H., et al. (2008). "Mortality and causes of death in autism spectrum disorders: an update." *Autism* 12(4): 403-14. Epub 2008/06/27.**

In: Advances in Autism Spectrum Disorder ... ISBN: 978-1-62257-058-4
Editors: R. L. Jackson and A. C. Lee

Chapter 3

2009 Summary of Advances in Autism Spectrum Disorder Research*

The Interagency Autism Coordinating Committee

About the IACC

The Interagency Autism Coordinating Committee (IACC) was established by Congress under the Combating Autism Act of 2006 (CAA) to provide advice to the Secretary of Health and Human Services (HHS) and coordinate all efforts within HHS concerning autism spectrum disorders (ASD).

As mandated by law, the IACC has a membership composed of federal officials from agencies involved in autism research and services and public members, including people with ASD, parents of children and adults with ASD, and members of the autism advocacy and research community. The diversity of the committee ensures that a broad range of views and opinions is reflected and discussed in a public forum.

Under the CAA, the IACC is required to: (1) Develop and annually update a strategic plan for ASD research, (2) develop and annually update a summary of advances in ASD research, and (3) monitor federal activities related to ASD.

In completing the first IACC Strategic Plan for Autism Spectrum Disorder Research in 2009 and releasing the first update of the plan in 2010, the IACC has laid out a framework for the pursuit of critical biomedical and services

* This is an edited, reformatted and augmented version of The Interagency Autism Coordinating Committee publication, dated 2009.

research. Through activities such as public meetings and workshops, publication of an annual Summary of Advances in ASD Research, dissemination of information regarding ASD research and IACC activities, gathering of public input and coordination of federal activities related to autism, the IACC continues in its effort to provide guidance to the Department of Health and Human Services and to reach out to the broader autism community to find ways to work together to help people with autism and their families. For more information about the IACC, see: www.iacc.hhs.gov.

THE 2009 IACC SUMMARY OF ADVANCES IN AUTISM SPECTRUM DISORDER RESEARCH

Introduction

Each year the members of the Interagency Autism Coordinating Committee identify recent research findings that made the most impact on the field. For the 2009 Summary of Advances, the IACC selected and summarized 20 studies that gave significant insight into the prevalence of autism spectrum disorder, the biology of the disorder, potential risk factors, and possible interventions. These articles were the top selections from a pool of 63 peer-reviewed articles published in 2009 that were nominated by the committee to reflect the most important work in biomedical and services research for ASD during the year — work that is critical to understanding the disorder and addressing the needs of people with ASD and their families. (Articles appear in alphabetical order by first author. A full reference list is included at the end of the document.)

Articles Selected for the 2009 Summary of Advances

Medication and Parent Training in Children with Pervasive Developmental Disorders and Serious Behavior Problems: Results from a Randomized Clinical Trial – Aman, et al. Journal of the American Academy of Child and Adolescent Psychiatry. December 2009

Training parents to use behavior management techniques, in combination with medication, reduces serious behavioral problems in children with ASD and related disorders when compared to medication use alone. Researchers randomly assigned 124 children, ages 4 to 13, into two groups – both groups received the antipsychotic risperidone, but in one group, parents received a structured training program teaching them to manage their children's severely disruptive and noncompliant behavior. Risperidone has been shown to reduce tantrums, aggression, and self-injury in children with autism; however, the drug can have side effects like significant weight gain and related health problems. The results of the study showed that while both groups of children improved over the six-month trial, the children whose parents had also received training (over an average of 11 sessions) showed a greater decrease in behavioral problems. These children were also taking a lower dose of risperidone at the end of the trial than the children being treated solely with medication (1.98 mg vs. 2.26 mg/daily). The authors noted that the benefits of actively engaging parents in treatment seemed to increase over time, further supporting the power of parent training. Future studies will evaluate whether the benefits of parent training continue into the future and whether younger children benefit as well. Based on the positive findings of this study, it may be beneficial to provide parent training through schools and community clinics.

Association of Family History of Autoimmune Diseases and Autism Spectrum Disorders – Atladóttir, et al. Pediatrics. August 2009

Mothers with rheumatoid arthritis or celiac disease, both classified as autoimmune disorders, are more likely to have children with ASD, based on a study of about 690,000 Danish children. Children with a family history of type 1 diabetes, another autoimmune disorder, are also more likely to have autism that is recognized in infancy. Researchers confirmed the results of earlier studies showing that family autoimmune disorders – disorders caused by an abnormal immune response against the body's own cells -- are linked to autism risk. While maternal rheumatoid arthritis and family history of type 1 diabetes were both known autism risk factors, the association between celiac disease and ASD was a new finding. Researchers looked at all children born in Denmark between 1993 and 2004 and identified children with an ASD diagnosis using the Danish National Psychiatric Registry. They then assessed the rate and type of autoimmune disorders found in the children's immediate family. To explain their findings, the authors hypothesize that the genes involved in autoimmune disorders may also contribute to ASD. There is also evidence that women with rheumatoid arthritis may produce antibodies during pregnancy that affect fetal brain development. Further research is necessary to explore these hypotheses.

Genome-Wide Analyses of Exonic Copy Number Variants in a Family-Based Study Point to Novel Autism Susceptibility Genes – Bucan, et al. Plos Genetics. June 2009

A study of more than 900 families with multiple cases of ASD revealed new autism risk genes and adds to what is known about the genetics of autism. The researchers identified 150 rare genetic variants found in two or more unrelated people with ASD, but not in typically developing individuals. Twenty-seven of these variants were also found in a separate group of people with ASD. These submicroscopic deletions and insertions of DNA, called copy number variants (CNV), were noted in genes that have been identified in other studies, such as neurexin 1 (NRXN1), which encodes a synaptic protein, and genes in the 15q11-q13 region of chromosome 15, including UBE3A, which encodes a ubiquitin-related enzyme. The study also implicated new genes, such as BZRAP1 (benzodiazepine receptor peripheral associated protein), which is involved in regulating the transmission of nerve impulses across the synapse. The researchers additionally noted finding abnormalities in a novel gene called MDGA2 gene in people with ASD (MAM domain containing glycosylphosphatidylinositol anchor 2), which is similar to another neuronal gene that has been implicated in mental retardation and autism. Overall, several of the genes identified produce proteins that allow the synapse – the junction through which neurons communicate – to function. Hundreds of rare genetic variants appeared only once in the study, underscoring the complexity of the genetics involved in ASD. However, greater understanding of the genetics underlying ASD could eventually lead to therapeutics that target specific genes and their pathways.

Prevalence of Autism Spectrum Disorders – Autism and Developmental Disabilities Monitoring Network, United States, 2006 – Centers for Disease Control and Prevention. Morbidity and Mortality Weekly Report (MMWR) Surveillance Summaries. December 2009

About one percent of 8-year-olds in the United States have an autism spectrum disorder, according to a CDC study of children in 2006 that was released in December 2009. This is a 57 percent increase from the rate of 1 in 150 children found in 2002 using the same research methods, although it is unclear how much of the increase results from better diagnosis and increased awareness. Similar to previous studies, boys were four times as likely to be affected as girls, with 1 in 70 boys receiving a diagnosis. Black or Hispanic children were less likely to have ASD than their white peers, but more research is needed to determine how much of the disparity may result from lower rates of diagnosis in these communities rather than lower rates of autism itself. Investigators analyzed the available medical records and school records of about 300,000 children across the US at 11 sites in the Autism and Developmental Disabilities Monitoring Network. ASD rates ranged across the sites between a high of 1 in 80 children in Arizona and Missouri to a low of 1 in 240 children in Florida. The study also showed that while children are being diagnosed slightly earlier than in 2002, the majority of children are not diagnosed until 3 1/2 to 5 years of age – a significant delay considering that most had concerns about their development documented in their records before their third birthday.

Autism Genome-Wide Copy Number Variation Reveals Ubiquitin and Neuronal Genes – Glessner, et al. Nature. May 2009

In the past few years, scientists studying autism have become very interested in a specific type of genetic variation caused by submicroscopic DNA deletions or duplications. Known as copy number variants (CNV), these mutations seem to occur more frequently in people with ASD and are yielding clues about the genetic basis of the disorder. For example, a 2008 study found that people with copy number variants in a region of chromosome 16 are likely to develop ASD. (This chromosomal region includes genes that appear to be related to neurodevelopment and brain function.) Now, a study of CNVs across the entire ASD genome has identified a cellular pathway known as the 'ubiquitin pathway' as potentially playing a role in ASD. This pathway is involved in altering protein function and acts as a 'filtration system' by removing unused or damaged proteins from the cell. The study, published in *Nature* in April 2009, also revealed variants in genes that had previously been identified in other studies, such as neurexin 1 (NRNX1) and contactin 4 (CNTN4). These genes code for proteins that help neurons adhere to one another and create synaptic connections, which are necessary for communication between neurons. Other genes with the similar functions, neuroligin 1 (NLGN1) and astrotactin 2 (ASTN2), were also newly implicated. The authors hypothesize that the two different types of gene networks identified in the study (ubiquitin-related and synaptic) may interact within the brain. They also note that while the CNVs found in the study are only present in a small percentage of people with ASD, they reveal important gene networks that may contribute to the disorder. Understanding the genetics of ASD may help researchers to categorize the disorder into subtypes and could eventually lead to the development of therapeutics targeting specific biological pathways.

Genomic and Epigenomic Evidence for Oxytocin Receptor Deficiency in Autism – Gregory, et al. BMC Medicine. October 2009

Oxytocin is a hormone believed to be involved in social behaviors such as recognition, bonding, and trust, as well as anxiety and repetitive behaviors. Acting primarily in the brain, early studies have suggested that oxytocin may play a role in ASD and some have suggested supplementing levels of the hormone as a potential treatment. A study published in *BMC Medicine* further supports the role of oxytocin receptors, which allow oxytocin to bind to neurons, in ASD. After comparing the complete genomes of 119 people who came from families with multiple cases of autism, researchers found one boy with ASD who was missing one copy of the oxytocin receptor gene (OXTR). His mother was missing one copy of the gene as well and showed symptoms of obsessive-compulsive disorder. Although his sibling with ASD was not missing the oxytocin receptor gene, the researchers found evidence suggesting that epigenetic changes —changes which can alter the expression of the gene without changing its basic DNA —could be the cause. These epigenetic changes can be caused by environmental factors and most commonly result from chemical entities called methyl groups attaching to points on the DNA helix. These methyl groups are read and, as a result, the gene is "turned off" (silenced) or "turned on" (activated). After examining levels of methylation in the sibling, it was found that there was increased methylation in a region that regulates the activity of the OXTR gene, suggesting that the gene was effectively silenced. The researchers also found evidence of epigenetic changes to elements that regulate OXTR in the blood and brain tissue of other people with ASD. This research provides more evidence that OXTR and the signaling pathway for oxytocin are involved in the disorder. This could potential give rise to therapeutics in the future, based on what researchers have discovered about the role of oxytocin in ASD.

Risk of Autism and Increasing Maternal and Paternal Age in a Large North American Population – Grether, et al. American Journal of Epidemiology. November 2009

Older mothers and older fathers are more likely to have a child with ASD when compared to younger parents, according to a study of 7.5 million children born in California from 1989 - 2002. While previous studies had shown a link between a father's age and autism risk, studies on the effect of a mother's age were not as conclusive. This study found that for every ten-year increase in a mother's age, her risk of having a child with ASD rose by 38 percent, independent of her partner's age. Each ten-year increase in a father's age raised his risk by 22 percent. This effect was seen in all races and ethnicities and was not affected by the baby's birth weight or gestational age. Parents' age had a greater affect on autism risk in first-born children than children born later. More research is necessary to understand why older parents are more likely to have children with ASD, but the authors hypothesize that a number of factors that impact older women may play a role, including hormonal changes that could affect fetal brain development, increased use of assisted reproductive technologies, age-related genetic changes, and the cumulative effect of exposures to environmental toxins. Older men are known to have accumulated a greater number of spontaneous genetic mutations in their sperm over time, which could increase the chances of having a child with ASD. More research is needed to understand autism risk factors and ultimately to communicate them to the public.

Representation of Internal Models of Action in the Autistic Brain – Haswell, et al. Nature Neuroscience. August 2009

Whenever a person decides to perform a movement, such as lifting his arm, the brain creates a model to predict what kind of sensory information will result. This model gives the person a sense of how the orientation of his arm will feel in relationship to his body, for example. Researchers have found that people with ASD are over-reliant on this sensory feedback (also called "proprioceptive information"), and that greater reliance is linked to greater levels of social impairment and poorer imitation skills. During the study, children were asked to manipulate a robotic arm to move a cursor to a target, "capturing" animals projected onto a screen if the child was quick and accurate enough. Children with ASD and typically developing children were trained on the robotic arm. After the training round, the handle for the robotic arm was moved, making it necessary for the children to readjust to the new positioning. The study revealed that children with ASD were over-reliant on their mental model of how their arm should feel in relationship to their body during the task. They were unable to use visual cues and adjust to the new positioning like their typically developing peers. These findings could explain in part why children with ASD often have issues with motor control and imitation, and may help to develop methods for improving motor skills in the future.

Incidence of Gastrointestinal Symptoms in Children with Autism: A Population-Based Study – Ibrahim, et al. Pediatrics. August 2009

The first long-term study of gastrointestinal (GI) issues in children with ASD found no difference in the frequency of symptoms when compared with typically developing children. While the issue remains a contentious one, this research adds to a body of evidence that GI disorders are no more frequent in children with ASD than they are in the general population. In the study, researchers tracked all the residents of Olmsted County, Minnesota who were younger than 21 years of age between 1976 and 1997. Within this group, there were 124 children who were diagnosed with ASD. The researchers followed these children, along with typically developing children of the same age and gender, until they were about 18 years old, tracking their gastrointestinal symptoms over many years. They found no difference between the two groups in overall incidence of GI symptoms or specific GI disorders. Although children with ASD were more likely to have constipation or feeding issues such as food selectivity, the authors suggest that these problems resulted from ASD-related behaviors rather than from true GI disorders. They conclude that although there may be subgroups of children with ASD who suffer from concurrent GI disorders that contribute to their behavior, this study suggests that in general, GI disorders are not more common in children with ASD than they are in typically developing children. They caution against the indiscriminate use of restrictive diets, vitamin and mineral supplements, and other related treatments for children with ASD, noting that these alternative treatments should only be used on a case-by-case basis for children with a diagnosed GI disorder.

Diagnostic Change and the Increased Prevalence of Autism – King and Bearman. International Journal of Epidemiology. October 2009

While autism prevalence has increased dramatically in the last 30 years, it is unclear how much of the increase can be explained by changes to diagnostic criteria and guidelines. After creating a statistical model based on the analysis of service records, researchers estimated that more than one-quarter (26.4%) of the increase in California since 1992 can be explained by a change in diagnosis among a specific group —people initially diagnosed with mental retardation whose diagnosis was later changed to autism. Researchers examined the case records of more than 7,000 people with ASD born before 1987 who were enrolled with the California Department of Developmental Services between 1992 and 2005. They paid particular attention to a group of patients who were initially diagnosed with mental retardation and then received an alternate or additional diagnosis of autism. After analysis, the researchers found that patients were much likelier to acquire an autism diagnosis after changes to the Diagnostic and Statistical Manual of Mental Disorders (DSM), or other diagnostic guidelines. There have been multiple changes to the DSM definition of autism since 1987, most significantly when the fourth edition was published in 1994. The authors conclude that changes in practices for diagnosing autism have had a substantial effect on the overall autism rate. While the shift in diagnosis from mental retardation to autism accounts for one-quarter of the increase, the reasons for the remaining 75 percent are still unexplained. Understanding the multiple factors that are influencing the increase in ASD may ultimately help to identify the underlying causes.

Two-Year Olds with Autism Orient to Non-Social Contingencies Rather Than Biological Motion – Klin, et al. Nature. May 2009

People with ASD tend to fixate on other's mouths when they speak rather than their eyes. Now a study published in *Nature* may explain why – the synchronization between mouth movements and speech are compelling for people with the disorder. In a study of toddlers, when presented with a range of possible cartoons to observe, children with ASD were preoccupied with cartoons where motion synchronized with sound, such as dots colliding to a produce a clapping sound. On the other hand, typically developing children were equally interested in cartoons where motion-sound synchrony was not as strong. The researchers studied the toddlers' eye movements while watching animations of people moving that had been reduced to points of light at each joint. Even with only a set of moving dots, young children without ASD are able to identify biological motion, such as a person walking, and are naturally drawn to it. The children with ASD showed no preference for biological motion over other types of movement, but were fascinated by animation where sound and motion synchronized. This is a likely explanation for why people with ASD favor the mouth over the eyes during a conversation. Understanding this tendency may help to develop future interventions.

Prevalence of Parent-Reported Diagnosis of Autism Spectrum Disorder Among Children in the US, 2007 – Kogan, et al. Pediatrics. November 2009

A 2007 survey of parents across the US, called the National Survey of Children's Health (NSCH), showed a similarly increased rate of ASD as the CDC surveillance study (CDC, 2009) published soon after. Parents who participated in the NCSH were asked whether their child had ever been diagnosed with ASD by a doctor or other health professional. They were then asked if their child currently had ASD. Based on the number of parents who said that their child had been diagnosed and still held the diagnosis, researchers estimated that ASD occurs in about 1 in 91 children in the US, slightly higher than the rate of 1 in 110 children found in the CDC study. Similar to other studies, boys were four times as likely to have ASD as girls and white children were more likely to be affected than black or multi-racial children. Interestingly, nearly 40 percent of children who had been diagnosed with ASD in the past no longer had the disorder, according to their parents. Black children were more likely than white children to have reportedly lost their diagnosis. The authors note that the number of children losing their diagnosis could be inflated —children who were suspected to have ASD but later found not to after subsequent assessments would be included in this group. It is also possible that children with developmental delays, mental retardation, or learning disabilities were initially classified as having ASD to obtain needed services. Unfortunately, these hypotheses cannot be tested using the data collected in this study. This study does give more evidence that the rate of ASD is increasing. Surveillance efforts such as these are critical to determining prevalence and providing information for communities when planning for services.

Racial/Ethnic Disparities in the Identification of Children with Autism Spectrum Disorders – Mandell, et al. American Journal of Public Health. March 2009

Studies have shown that ASD is often diagnosed long after symptoms have appeared or is misdiagnosed as another disorder. Unfortunately, these delays and errors seem to be even more frequent in racial and ethnic minorities. A study published in the March issue of the *American Journal of Public Health* revealed that black and Hispanic children with ASD were less likely to have been diagnosed by a medical professional than were white children. This was also true of children who identified their race/ethnicity as "other." Most of the Asian and Hispanic children who failed to be diagnosed with ASD also had an intellectual disability (IQ<70), which can complicate ASD diagnosis. However, black children were less likely to be diagnosed regardless of whether or not they had an intellectual disability. Researchers screened health care and education records from about 2,600 eight-year-olds at sites across the US involved in the CDC's Autism and Development Disabilities Monitoring (ADDM) network. Using the records, experienced clinical reviewers assessed whether the child had documented symptoms that met the criteria for ASD and whether an official diagnosis had been made. In total, only 58 percent of children in the study meeting the case definition of ASD had received a diagnosis. In addition to minority groups, girls were also significantly less likely to receive a diagnosis when compared to boys. This was also true of children whose mothers had not completed high school. The authors note that mothers with greater education may be more aware that a diagnosis is necessary to receive educational services. The significant racial and ethnic disparities shown in the study support the need for continued professional education for clinicians to improve ASD identification in children.

Abnormal Behavior in a Chromosome-Engineered Mouse Model for Human 15q11-13 Duplication Seen in Autism – Nakatani, et al. Cell. June 2009

Researchers bred mice to have a genetic abnormality that is analogous to one frequently seen in people with ASD and found that the mice showed similar patterns of inflexible behavior, impaired social skills, and anxiety seen in people with the disorder. The mice were engineered to have a duplication on mouse chromosome 7 that bears strong similarity to a particular region of human chromosome 15 —15q11-13 — which has been linked to autism. In the study, researchers found that animals that had inherited the engineered duplication from their fathers showed behaviors characteristic of ASD. These mice showed impaired social abilities, choosing not to interact when introduced to a stranger mouse, and were less able to adapt to changes in mazes than other mice. They were also more likely to show anxiety or depression, based on their reactions to forced swim tests and their increased distress calls when separated from their mother as pups. These findings give evidence that duplications to this particular genomic region can contribute to the behaviors typical of ASD. In addition, this research represents an advance in the development of animal models of autism that display both genetic and behavioral similarities to the disorder in humans. Animal models such as this one will be critical for future research into the underlying biology of ASD.

Autism and Other Neuropsychiatric Symptoms Are Prevalent in Individuals with MECP2 Duplication Syndrome – Ramocki, et al. Annals of Neurology. December 2009

Boys with a rare and potentially fatal brain disorder caused by an additional copy of the MECP2 gene are very likely to also have autism, based on a study published in the *Annals of Neurology*. Genetic variation in the MECP2 gene (methyl-CpG-binding protein 2) is known to cause Rett syndrome, a neurodevelopmental disorder on the autism spectrum that appears in girls. Researchers set out to find if the duplication of this gene would cause autism in males and lesser ASD symptoms in females. MECP2 codes for a protein which is essential for brain development and is thought to be involved in the silencing ("turning off") of several other genes. Boys with an additional copy of MECP2 develop MeCP2 Duplication Syndrome, a recently discovered disorder marked by severe intellectual disability, muscle weakness, and seizures. Researchers studied eight families with MECP2 duplication (9 males and 9 females) and found that all of the boys had classic autism and mental retardation. Their mothers, who were shown to be carriers of the disorder, all experienced psychiatric symptoms, including anxiety, depression, and compulsive behavior. Four of the seven mothers were on the autism spectrum. This study supports genetic testing for MECP2 duplication in boys with autism and mental retardation. If the disorder is identified, the entire family may benefit from genetic counseling – mothers are likely to be carriers and siblings may also be affected. This study also suggests that since duplication of the MECP2 gene is so strongly linked to development of autism in humans, that study of MECP2 function in animal models may reveal critical new insights into how autism develops.

Timing of Identification Among Children with an Autism Spectrum Disorder: Findings from a Population-Based Surveillance Study – Shattuck, et al. Journal of the American Academy of Child and Adolescent Psychiatry. May 2009

A large national study of children with ASD revealed that the median age of diagnosis was nearly 6 years old and more than one-quarter of the children were not diagnosed until age 8. Experienced clinicians can identify autism between 2 and 3 years of age, so these statistics show that diagnosis is significantly delayed in most cases. With later diagnosis, children with ASD miss a critical window for early intervention, which has been shown to have a profound impact on development. Researchers reviewed the medical records and education records, when available, of the approximately 2,600 children included in the 2002 ADDM surveillance study. An analysis of the data showed that boys were more likely to be diagnosed at a younger age, as were children with intellectual disabilities (IQ<70), and those who had experienced regression. The authors noted that the gender differences in diagnosis could stem from cultural biases about what constitutes normal behavior for girls – for, example shyness may be more socially acceptable. There was no difference in age of diagnosis across races after adjusting for other factors. This study shows significant delays between the age at which diagnosis is possible and when it is actually taking place. Researchers need to conduct research to understand the consequences of late identification and develop methods to improve the timing of diagnosis. Future efforts should also focus on identifying ASD in school-aged children who may not have been diagnosed earlier, according to the study authors.

Partial Reversal of Rett Syndrome-Like Symptoms in MECP2 Mutant Mice – Tropea, et al. Proceedings of the National Academy of Sciences USA. February 2009

Researchers were able to reverse some of the symptoms of Rett syndrome in a mouse model through daily injections of insulin-like growth factor-1 (IGF-1), a hormone involved in childhood growth. Rett syndrome, classified as part of the autism spectrum, occurs almost exclusively in girls and is caused by mutations to the MeCP2 gene on the X chromosome. Researchers bred mice with the same genetic abnormality and, as a result, showed similar symptoms to humans with Rett syndrome: lethargy, abnormal breathing, irregular heartbeat, smaller brains, and shortened lifespan. Researchers also observed that the MeCP2 mutant mice had immature synapses, which are necessary for sending signals throughout the brain. Previous research had suggested that one of the target genes regulated by MeCP2 is brain-derived neurotrophic factor (BDNF), which is a growth factor protein that stimulates growth and differentiation of neurons and synapses. Because BDNF does not easily cross the blood-brain barrier, researchers decided to try to see if another related growth factor called insulin growth factor -1 (IGF-1) might be able to reverse Rett syndrome symptoms in the mouse model. The researchers found that after daily injections of IGF-1, the mice were more active, their breathing and heart rate normalized, and they lived longer than the MeCP2 mice that did not receive the treatment. Importantly, their brain weight increased and they showed signs that their synapses were maturing — the number of dendritic spines, projections on the neuron used to send and receive electrical signals, also increased. The authors note that while the effects of IGF-1 are significant, the mice still develop the full range of symptoms and die prematurely. More research is needed to understand how IGF-1 works to reduce symptoms of Rett syndrome, but this study has exciting implications for potential treatments.

Common Genetic Variants on 5p14.1 Associate with Autism Spectrum Disorders – Wang, et al. Nature. May 2009

Researchers have identified several genomic variants commonly found in people with ASD near two genes on chromosome 5. The strong association of these variants with cases of ASD suggests that they confer risk for the disorder. While many other genetic variants linked to ASD have been identified to date, individually those variants are rare, accounting for only a fraction of cases.

This study is the first to find common variants associated with ASD, and came after examining the full genomes of 10,000 people with ASD, family members, and volunteers. The two genes implicated, cadherin 9 (CDH9) and cadherin 10 (CDH10), code for proteins that are embedded in the surface of neurons and allow them to adhere to one another. The authors believe that the newly identified variants may impact the function of these two nearby genes, disrupting neural connections being formed in the developing brain. This finding converges with other recent studies that have implicated genes with a similar function. Results of the study were replicated in two other sample groups. Genome-wide studies allow an extremely comprehensive look at the genetic risk factors for ASD. Together with studies of environmental risk factors and changes to gene expression, scientists will be better able to understand the basis of ASD, which may ultimate result in new treatments and strategies for prevention.

A Genome-Wide Linkage and Association Scan Reveals Novel Loci for Autism – Weiss, et al. Nature. October 2009

While past studies have had limited success identifying autism risk genes that could account for the majority of cases, new technologies that allow researchers to scan a person's entire genetic make-up are leading to new breakthroughs.

One such genome-wide study of more than 1,500 people with ASD revealed that genetic abnormalities at a region on chromosome 5 — 5p15 — are linked to the disorder.

A gene in this region, semaphorin-5A (SEMA5A), is involved in guiding the neuron's axon during early brain development (the axon is the projection from the neuron that conducts the impulses used to communicate with other cells). Researchers found decreased levels of the protein produced by SEMA5A in the brains of people with ASD, which suggests that the gene is involved in ASD.

In addition to the region on chromosome 5, two other locations were found to be associated with ASD: regions on chromosome 6 (6q27) and chromosome 20 (20p13).

By identifying genetic regions and specific genes related to ASD, researchers may be able to one day conduct genetic screening for the disorder to improve diagnosis and develop targeted treatments.

Clinical Assessment and Management of Toddlers with Suspected Autism Spectrum Disorder: Insights from Studies of High-Risk Infants – Zwaigenbaum, et al. Pediatrics. May 2009

With the increased emphasis on early detection and the recommendations from the American Academy of Pediatrics that all 18- and 24-month-olds be screened for ASD, it is important for clinicians to understand how the diagnostic criteria for ASD can be applied to children in this age group and which methods and tools can be used to provide the most reliable diagnosis. An article published in Pediatrics addresses what is known about the early signs of ASD, best practices for diagnosis in very young children, and available interventions. Studies of infants who have an older sibling with ASD show that developmental delays related to the disorder can be detected from 12 to 18 months of age. These signs could include a lack of eye contact, delayed motor skills, repetitive actions with toys, or a lack of babbling. However, doctors are faced with trying to diagnose ASD with assessments that may not be useful for children under two years of age. Research shows that fewer than 1 in 5 children diagnosed with ASD at 20 to 24 months of age were correctly identified by the Checklist for Autism in Toddlers (CHAT) at 18 months. Even if a diagnosis is suspected, clinicians have difficulty recommending appropriate interventions for children less than two years of age. It has not been established whether interventions designed for pre-school age children are beneficial for toddlers. The authors advise clinicians to follow up with parents who express concerns about their toddler's development, referring them for additional evaluation and early intervention services when appropriate. Ongoing research will help to expand the options for diagnosing and treating very young children suspected to have ASD.

REFERENCES

Aman MG, McDougle CJ, Scahill L, Handen B, Arnold LE, Johnson C, Stigler KA, Bearss K, Butter E, Swiezy NB, Sukhodolsky DD, Ramadan Y, Pozdol SL, Nikolov R, Lecavalier L, Kohn AE, Koenig K, Hollway JA, Korzekwa P, Gavaletz A, Mulick JA, Hall KL, Dziura J, Ritz L, Trollinger S, Yu S, Vitiello B, Wagner A; the Research Units on Pediatric Psychopharmacology Autism Network. Medication and parent training in children with pervasive developmental disorders and serious behavior problems: results from a randomized clinical trial. *J. Am. Acad. Child Adolesc. Psychiatry*. 2009 Dec;48(12):1143- 1154.

Atladóttir HO, Pedersen MG, Thorsen P, Mortensen PB, Deleuran B, Eaton WW, Parner ET. Association of family history of autoimmune diseases and autism spectrum disorders. *Pediatrics.* 2009 Aug;124(2):687-94.

Bucan M, Abrahams BS, Wang K, Glessner JT, Herman EI, Sonnenblick LI, Alvarez Retuerto AI, Imielinski M, Hadley D, Bradfield JP, Kim C, Gidaya NB, Lindquist I, Hutman T, Sigman M, Kustanovich V, Lajonchere CM, Singleton A, Kim J, Wassink TH, McMahon WM, Owley T, Sweeney JA, Coon H, Nurnberger JI, Li M, Cantor RM, Minshew NJ, Sutcliffe JS, Cook EH, Dawson G, Buxbaum JD, Grant SF, Schellenberg GD, Geschwind DH, Hakonarson H. Genome-wide analyses of exonic copy number variants in a family-based study point to novel autism susceptibility genes. *PLoS Genet.* 2009 Jun;5(6):e1000536.

Centers for Disease Control and Prevention (CDC); Autism and Developmental Disabilities Monitoring Network Surveillance Year 2006 Principal Investigators. Prevalence of autism spectrum disorders - Autism and Developmental Disabilities Monitoring Network, United States, 2006. *MMWR Surveill. Summ*. 2009 Dec 18;58(10):1-20.

Glessner JT, Wang K, Cai G, Korvatska O, Kim CE, Wood S, Zhang H, Estes A, Brune CW, Bradfield JP, Imielinski M, Frackelton EC, Reichert J, Crawford EL, Munson J, Sleiman PM, Chiavacci R, Annaiah K, Thomas K, Hou C, Glaberson W, Flory J, Otieno F, Garris M, Soorya L, Klei L, Piven J, Meyer KJ, Anagnostou E, Sakurai T, Game RM, Rudd DS, Zurawiecki D, McDougle CJ, Davis LK, Miller J, Posey DJ, Michaels S, Kolevzon A, Silverman JM, Bernier R, Levy SE, Schultz RT, Dawson G, Owley T, McMahon WM, Wassink TH, Sweeney JA, Nurnberger JI, Coon H, Sutcliffe JS, Minshew NJ, Grant SF, Bucan M, Cook EH, Buxbaum JD, Devlin B, Schellenberg GD, Hakonarson H. Autism genome-wide copy number variation reveals ubiquitin and neuronal genes. *Nature*. 2009 May 28;459(7246):569-73.

Gregory SG, Connelly JJ, Towers AJ, Johnson J, Biscocho D, Markunas CA, Lintas C, Abramson RK, Wright HH, Ellis P, Langford CF, Worley G, Delong GR, Murphy SK, Cuccaro ML, Persico A, Pericak-Vance MA. Genomic and epigenetic evidence for oxytocin receptor deficiency in autism. *BMC Med.* 2009 Oct 22;7:62.

Grether JK, Anderson MC, Croen LA, Smith D, Windham GC. Risk of autism and increasing maternal and paternal age in a large North American population. *Am. J .Epidemiol.* 2009 Nov 1;170(9):1118-26.

Haswell CC, Izawa J, Dowell LR, Mostofsky SH, Shadmehr R. Representation of internal models of action in the autistic brain. *Nat. Neurosci.* 2009 Aug;12(8):970-2.

Ibrahim SH, Voigt RG, Katusic SK, Weaver AL, Barbaresi WJ. Incidence of gastrointestinal symptoms in children with autism: a population-based study. *Pediatrics.* 2009 Aug;124(2):680-6.

King M, Bearman P. Diagnostic change and the increased prevalence of autism. *Int. J. Epidemiol.* 2009 Oct;38(5):1224-34.

Klin A, Lin DJ, Gorrindo P, Ramsay G, Jones W. Two-year-olds with autism orient to non-social contingencies rather than biological motion. *Nature.* 2009 May 14;459(7244):257-61.

Kogan MD, Blumberg SJ, Schieve LA, Boyle CA, Perrin JM, Ghandour RM, Singh GK, Strickland BB, Trevathan E, van Dyck PC. Prevalence of parent-reported diagnosis of autism spectrum disorder among children in the US, 2007. *Pediatrics.* 2009 Nov;124(5):1395-403.

Mandell DS, Wiggins LD, Carpenter LA, Daniels J, DiGuiseppi C, Durkin MS, Giarelli E, Morrier MJ, Nicholas JS, Pinto-Martin JA, Shattuck PT, Thomas KC, Yeargin-Allsopp M, Kirby RS. Racial/ethnic disparities in the identification of children with autism spectrum disorders. *Am. J. Public Health.* 2009 Mar;99(3):493-8.

Nakatani J, Tamada K, Hatanaka F, Ise S, Ohta H, Inoue K, Tomonaga S, Watanabe Y, Chung YJ, Banerjee R, Iwamoto K, Kato T, Okazawa M, Yamauchi K, Tanda K, Takao K, Miyakawa T, Bradley A, Takumi T. Abnormal behavior in a chromosome-engineered mouse model for human 15q11-13 duplication seen in autism. *Cell.* 2009 Jun 26;137(7):1235-46.

Ramocki MB, Peters SU, Tavyev YJ, Zhang F, Carvalho CM, Schaaf CP, Richman R, Fang P, Glaze DG, Lupski JR, Zoghbi HY. Autism and other neuropsychiatric symptoms are prevalent in individuals with MeCP2 duplication syndrome. *Ann. Neurol.* 2009 Dec;66(6):771-82.

Shattuck PT, Durkin M, Maenner M, Newschaffer C, Mandell DS, Wiggins L, Lee LC, Rice C, Giarelli E, Kirby R, Baio J, Pinto-Martin J, Cuniff C. Timing of identification among children with an autism spectrum disorder: findings from a population-based surveillance study. *J. Am. Acad. Child Adolesc. Psychiatry.* 2009 May;48(5):474-83.

Tropea D, Giacometti E, Wilson NR, Beard C, McCurry C, Fu DD, Flannery R, Jaenisch R, Sur M. Partial reversal of Rett Syndrome-like symptoms in MeCP2 mutant mice. *Proc. Natl. Acad. Sci. USA.* 2009 Feb 10;106(6):2029-34.

Wang K, Zhang H, Ma D, Bucan M, Glessner JT, Abrahams BS, Salyakina D, Imielinski M, Bradfield JP, Sleiman PM, Kim CE, Hou C, Frackelton E, Chiavacci R, Takahashi N, Sakurai T, Rappaport E, Lajonchere CM, Munson J, Estes A, Korvatska O, Piven J, Sonnenblick LI, Alvarez Retuerto AI, Herman EI, Dong H, Hutman T, Sigman M, Ozonoff S, Klin A, Owley T, Sweeney JA, Brune CW, Cantor RM, Bernier R, Gilbert JR, Cuccaro ML, McMahon WM, Miller J, State MW, Wassink TH, Coon H, Levy SE, Schultz RT, Nurnberger JI, Haines JL, Sutcliffe JS, Cook EH, Minshew NJ, Buxbaum JD, Dawson G, Grant SF, Geschwind DH, Pericak-Vance MA, Schellenberg GD, Hakonarson H. Common genetic variants on 5p14.1 associate with autism spectrum disorders. *Nature.* 2009 May 28;459(7246):528-33.

Weiss LA, Arking DE; Gene Discovery Project of Johns Hopkins & the Autism Consortium, Daly MJ, Chakravarti A. A genome-wide linkage and association scan reveals novel loci for autism. *Nature.* 2009 Oct 8;461(7265):802-8.

Zwaigenbaum L, Bryson S, Lord C, Rogers S, Carter A, Carver L, Chawarska K, Constantino J, Dawson G, Dobkins K, Fein D, Iverson J, Klin A, Landa R, Messinger D, Ozonoff S, Sigman M, Stone W, Tager-Flusberg H, Yirmiya N. Clinical assessment and management of toddlers with suspected autism spectrum disorder: insights from studies of high-risk infants. *Pediatrics.* 2009 May;123(5):1383-91.

In: Advances in Autism Spectrum Disorder ... ISBN: 978-1-62257-058-4
Editors: R. L. Jackson and A. C. Lee

Chapter 4

2010 SUMMARY OF ADVANCES IN AUTISM SPECTRUM DISORDER RESEARCH*

The Interagency Autism Coordinating Committee

ABOUT THE IACC

The Interagency Autism Coordinating Committee (IACC) was established by Congress under the Combating Autism Act of 2006 (CAA) to provide advice to the Secretary of Health and Human Services (HHS) and coordinate all efforts within HHS concerning autism spectrum disorders (ASD).

As mandated by law, the IACC has a membership composed of federal officials from agencies involved in autism research and services and public members, including people with ASD, parents of children and adults with ASD, and members of the autism advocacy and research community. The diversity of the committee ensures that a broad range of views and opinions is reflected and discussed in a public forum.

Under the CAA, the IACC is required to (1) develop and annually update a Strategic Plan for ASD research, (2) develop and annually update a summary of advances in ASD research, and (3) monitor federal activities related to ASD.

---

* This is an edited, reformatted and augmented version of The Interagency Autism Coordinating Committee Publication.

In developing and updating the *IACC Strategic Plan for Autism Spectrum Disorder Research*, first released in 2009 and subsequently updated in 2010 and 2011, the IACC has laid out a framework for the pursuit of critical biomedical and services research. Through activities such as public meetings and workshops, publication of an annual *Summary of Advances in ASD Research*, dissemination of information regarding ASD research and IACC activities, gathering of public input and coordination of Federal activities related to autism, the IACC continues in its effort to provide guidance to the Department of Health and Human Services and to reach out to the broader autism community to find ways to work together to help people with autism and their families. *For more information about the IACC, see www.iacc.hhs.gov.*

THE 2010 IACC SUMMARY OF ADVANCES IN AUTISM SPECTRUM DISORDER RESEARCH

Introduction

As part of the Combating Autism Act of 2006, the members of the Interagency Autism Coordinating Committee are required to develop an annual "Summary of Advances" to describe each year's top advances in autism spectrum disorder research.

These advances represent significant progress in the early diagnosis of ASD, understanding the complex biology of the disorder, and identifying potential risk factors.

They may also relate to work identifying effective treatments and services and studies of the national prevalence of ASD and necessary research infrastructure.

The 2010 Summary of Advances provides short, plain language synopses of the top twenty research breakthroughs selected by the committee from a pool of 64 peer-reviewed articles nominated by the members. Articles are grouped according to the questions of the IACC Strategic Plan for ASD Research (available at www.iacc.hhs.gov).

Citations for the articles selected for the Summary of Advances, as well as a complete listing of those nominated, are included at the end of the document.

ARTICLES SELECTED FOR THE 2010 SUMMARY OF ADVANCES

Question 1: Diagnosis - When Should I Be Concerned?

Implementing Developmental Screening and Referrals: Lessons Learned from a National Project

King TM, Tandon SD, Macias MM, Healy JA, Duncan PM, Swigonski NL, Skipper SM, Lipkin PH. Pediatrics. 2010 Feb;125(2):350-60.

In 2006, the American Academy of Pediatrics (AAP) issued guidelines on developmental surveillance and screening that included the recommendation that all children be screened for developmental delays at 9, 18, and 24 or 30 months of age.

In addition, children who were identified as being at risk should be referred for a detailed evaluation by a specialist and enrolled in early intervention services.

In an effort to improve the adoption of their guidelines, the AAP simultaneously launched a project to assess how well the guidelines were being implemented in 17 diverse clinical settings. The study found that while most pediatricians conducted the regular developmental screenings recommended by the AAP, there could be significant improvement in the issuing and tracking of referrals for children who fail screens. Based on patient records from the monitored sites, the practices were successful in screening over 85 percent of patients who returned for appointments at the recommended ages.

In phone interviews, individuals working at the practices reported that the high rate of screening was accomplished by delegating responsibilities among staff and actively monitoring whether screens had taken place. However, several sites had difficulty consistently screening children during busy periods or after periods of staff turnover.

Many practices also had difficulty issuing and tracking referrals for children who were deemed to be at risk for developmental delays – 39 percent of children who failed screens never received the recommended referrals to a specialist and an early intervention program. When tracking did take place, the clinicians found that many parents had not followed through with the referrals. Based on the project, the authors conclude that more focus should be placed on the referral process and communicating with families about the reasons for the referrals.

Consensus Statement: Chromosomal Microarray Is a First-Tier Clinical Diagnostic Test for Individuals with Developmental Disabilities or Congenital Anomalies

Miller DT, Adam MP, Aradhya S, Biesecker LG, Brothman AR, Carter NP, Church DM, Crolla JA, Eichler EE, Epstein CJ, Faucett WA, Feuk L, Friedman JM, Hamosh A, Jackson L, Kaminsky EB, Kok K, Krantz ID, Kuhn RM, Lee C, Ostell JM, Rosenberg C, Scherer SW, Spinner NB, Stavropoulos DJ, Tepperberg JH, Thorland EC, Vermeesch JR, Waggoner DJ, Watson MS, Martin CL, Ledbetter DH. Am J Hum Genet. 2010 May 14;86(5):749-64.

An international consortium of geneticists recommended that chromosomal microarray assessment (CMA) be used as the standard genetic test for diagnosing people with unexplained developmental or intellectual delay, autism spectrum disorders, or birth defects. Previously, a test developed in the 1970s called G-banded karyotyping was the standard assessment used, but a literature review conducted by the consortium showed that CMA has greater sensitivity, resulting in a greater likelihood of diagnosis (3% diagnosis rate using G-banded karyotyping compared to 15 – 20% using CMA). This is primarily because CMA has greater sensitivity for submicroscopic deletions and insertions of DNA known as copy number variations. Researchers were able to develop CMA after the Human Genome Project was completed in 2000, and it has become a commonly ordered test for patients with developmental concerns. However, formal best practice guidelines had yet to be issued recommending CMA as a first-tier diagnostic test. The consortium concluded that CMA should be used in place of G-banded karyotyping as the genetic test for patients with unexplained developmental or intellectual delay, autism spectrum disorder, or birth defects. G-banded karyotyping should only be used by those who have obvious chromosomal syndromes such as Down syndrome, a family history of chromosomal rearrangement, or a history of multiple miscarriages.

Automated Vocal Analysis of Naturalistic Recordings from Children with Autism, Language Delay, and Typical Development

Oller DK, Niyogi P, Gray S, Richards JA, Gilkerson J, Xu D, Yapanel U, Warren SF. Proc Natl Acad Sci U S A. 2010 Jul 27;107(30):13354-9.

Researchers have developed technology assessing patterns of vocalization that can distinguish children with ASD from others with a relatively high degree of accuracy. Using a lightweight recording device clipped to clothing, researchers captured 1,486 day-long recordings from children diagnosed with ASD, language delay, and those who were developing typically. The children in the study ranged from 10 months to 4 years of age. Investigators created a program that analyzes patterns of speech (or the cooing and babbling that precedes speech) and is able to distinguish children with ASD from their typically developing peers with 86 percent accuracy. Of those with developmental disorders, children with ASD were reliably distinguished from children with language delay with 70 percent accuracy. Vocalizations were assessed using 12 separate parameters but investigators found that the most important factor for identification was the child's ability to produce clear syllables through quick movements of the jaw and tongue. The authors discuss the potential for using automated analysis as a convenient and objective addition to diagnostic tests for ASD and language delay. Ultimately, vocal analysis could help to decrease the average age of diagnosis for children with ASD (reported to be about 4'A to 5'A years of age in the United States), allowing children to start interventions earlier. Future efforts will focus on fine-tuning the technology to better differentiate between different subgroups of language disorders.

A Prospective Study of the Emergence of Early Behavioral Signs of Autism

Ozonoff S, Iosif AM, Baguio F, Cook IC, Hill MM, Hutman T, Rogers SJ, Rozga A, Sangha S, Sigman M, Steinfeld MB, Young GS. J Am Acad Child Adolesc Psychiatry. 2010 Mar;49(3):256-66.e1-2.

The study found that children with ASD generally do not show signs of the disorder at six months of age but that a plateauing or loss of social skills is evident by the time they reach their first birthday. The finding suggests that behavioral symptoms of autism are not present at birth as hypothesized by the man who first identified ASD, Dr. Leo Kanner, but instead emerge after six months of age in most instances. The authors of the study note that there may be some cases where behavioral signs of ASD are present at six months of age or earlier but that this pattern of onset is probably less common than originally thought. The researchers reached these conclusions by comparing the social behavior of 25 infants who were ultimately diagnosed with ASD to that of 25 typically developing infants. Researchers observed the children at 6, 12, 18, 24, and 36 months of age and coded the frequency of specific types of social communication behavior (e.g., gazing at faces, social smiling, vocalizations directed at a listener, etc.). The children showed no difference in social behavior at 6 months of age but by 12 months, the majority of children with ASD had failed to gain new social skills or had lost previously acquired ones. Notably, the majority of children with ASD showed a gradual loss of specific social skills, particularly between 6 and 18 months of age. However, this subtle regression in development went unnoticed by most parents. This demonstrates a critical flaw in retrospective studies of onset using parent report. The authors note that the traditional models of autism (early onset of symptoms or dramatic regression after typical development) may not adequately portray how ASD emerges and suggest that additional models may need to be developed. Alternately, the onset of symptoms may be better represented by a continuum based on the amount and timing of regression.

Question 2: Biology - How Can I Understand What is Happening?

Evaluation, Diagnosis, and Treatment of Gastrointestinal Disorders in Individuals with ASDs: A Consensus Report

Buie T, Campbell DB, Fuchs, GJ 3rd, Furuta GT, Levy J, VandeWater J, Whitaker AH, Atkins D, Bauman ML, Beaudet AL, Carr EG, Gershon MD, Hyman SL, Jirapinyo P, Jyonouchi H, Kooros K, Kushak R, Levitt P, Levy SE, Lewis JD, Murray KF, Natowicz MR, Sabra A, Wershil BK, Weston SC, Zeltzer L, Winter H. Pediatrics. 2010 Jan;125(Suppl 1):S1 -S18.

Recommendations for Evaluation and Treatment of Common Gastrointestinal Problems in Children with ASDs

Buie T, Fuchs GJ 3rd, Furuta GT, Kooros K, Levy J, Lewis JD, Wershil BK, Winter H. Pediatrics. 2010 Jan;125(Suppl 1):S19-29.

A panel of experts reviewed the medical literature on ASD and gastrointestinal (GI) disorders and developed a consensus report (Buie, Cambell, Fuchs et al., 2010) and recommendations for evaluation, diagnosis, and treatment (Buie, Fuchs, Furuta et al., 2010). While GI issues are commonly reported among people with ASD, the actual rate of these co-occurring issues and the proper methods for diagnosis and treatment are not well understood. The panel reached a consensus that people with ASD who have GI symptoms should receive the same thorough evaluation as any other patient. In addition, the experts concluded that GI issues reported in people with ASD are also common to the general population and that there is not sufficient evidence of a GI disorder unique to people on the spectrum. Further, they stated that medical problems such as GI issues may manifest as behavioral problems in people with ASD and that the underlying cause may be difficult to diagnose, particularly if the person is non-verbal. It may be beneficial to coordinate behavioral and medical treatment simultaneously in these instances. The panel concluded that the bulk of the literature does not support the idea that diets restricting gluten and/or casein can lessen the symptoms of ASD. However, existing evidence has not ruled out the possibility that a particular subset may respond to a restricted diet. The panel advised those who choose to follow these diets to do so in consultation with a nutritionist. Currently, data do not support that intestinal inflammation, increased intestinal permeability (or "leaky gut"), food allergies, or immunological issues play a role in causing ASD. More research is needed to understand what, if any, part these issues play. Additionally, any future studies of ASD and GI should include genetic analysis to better define potential subgroups of individuals. Ultimately, researchers are working to gather enough information to develop evidence-based guidelines standardizing care for children with ASD who experience GI problems.

Describing the Brain in Autism in Five Dimensions – Magnetic Resonance Imaging-Assisted Diagnosis of Autism Spectrum Disorder Using a Multiparameter Classification Approach

Ecker C, Marquand A, Mourao-Miranda J, Johnston P, Daly EM, Brammer MJ, Maltezos S, Murphy CM, Robertson D, Williams SC, Murphy DG. J Neurosci. 2010 Aug11;30(32):10612-23.

Using magnetic resonance imaging (MRI), researchers were able to identify people with ASD by measuring subtle differences in brain structure. The investigators used a complex mathematical process to predict whether or not the person had ASD based on five dimensions of the brain selected for study by the researchers. These dimensions included both size (volume) and shape of various brain regions. The researchers found that no one structural feature could definitively identify whether a person had ASD, but when all five dimensions were taken together, they could distinguish people with ASD from typically developing individuals with up to 90 percent accuracy. The technique showed a false-positive rate (misdiagnosing ASD in a typically developing person) of about 20 percent, and ASD identification was more accurate when measures were taken from the left hemisphere of the brain. The authors discuss the theory that brain structure changes are more prominent in the left hemispheres of people with ASD, resulting in enhanced asymmetry between and the left and right halves of the brain. The researchers also tested how accurately their technique could distinguish people with ADHD from those with ASD and found that the algorithm misdiagnosed ASD in someone with ADHD 21 percent of the time. Future research will be needed to refine the technique, but the study demonstrates its potential as a valuable tool for diagnosing and understanding the biological underpinnings of ASD.

Mitochondrial Dysfunction in Autism

Giulivi C, Zhang YF, Omanska-Klusek A, Ross-Inta C, Wong S, Hertz-Picciotto I, Tassone F, Pessah IN. JAMA. 2010 Dec 1;304(21):2389-96.

A preliminary study found that children with classic autism were more likely to have impaired mitochondrial function and abnormalities in mitochondrial DNA when compared to their typically developing peers. Mitochondria supply energy to cells and have their own set of genetic instructions. Questions surrounding mitochondrial dysfunction and autism have long existed, and some have hypothesized that the inability to adequately fuel neurons could account for some of the cognitive issues associated with autism. Mitochondrial dysfunction has been linked to several other neurological disorders including Parkinson's disease, Alzheimer's disease, schizophrenia, and bipolar disorder. In the investigation, researchers randomly selected ten children with ASD participating in the Childhood Autism Risks from Genetics and Environment (CHARGE) study being conducted at the M.I.N.D. Institute in California and compared them with ten typically developing children also participating in the study. The investigators took blood samples from the children, who ranged from 2 to 5 years of age, and analyzed the mitochondria present in immune cells called lymphocytes. They found that the mitochondria in children with autism were consuming significantly less oxygen than controls, indicating lowered mitochondrial activity and decreased ability to supply energy to cells. Children with autism also had higher levels of pyruvate, the basic material mitochondria transform into energy, suggesting that they were unable to process pyruvate quickly enough to meet energy demands. Hydrogen peroxide levels in the mitochondria were also elevated, which could indicate higher levels of oxidative stress – an imbalance that results in cellular damage. Oxidative stress can cause mitochondria to produce extra copies of DNA, which was seen in half of children with autism. In addition, two of the ten children showed deletions in their mitochondrial DNA. The study provides evidence that mitochondrial dysfunction may be more common in children with autism and warrants further research.

Neural Signatures of Autism

Kaiser MD, Hudac CM, Shultz S, Lee SM, Cheung C, Berken AM, Deen B, Pitskel NB, Sugrue DR, Voos AC, Saulnier CA, Ventola P, Wolf JM, Klin A,

Vander Wyk BC, Pelphrey KA. Proc Natl Acad Sci U S A. 2010 Dec 7;107(49):21223-8.

Researchers have identified patterns of brain activity that are unique to people with autism spectrum disorder. These distinct patterns, also called neural signatures, may be useful in diagnosis and identifying subgroups of people with ASD. Using functional magnetic resonance imaging (fMRI), investigators performed scans of 62 children, 4 to 17 years of age, while they watched animations of biological motion (movements such as walking or running simplified to dots representing the major joints). Children in the study were diagnosed with ASD, typically developing, or siblings of children with ASD who did not have the diagnosis themselves. The study found that children with ASD showed less activity in certain brain regions when viewing the biological motion than did typically developing children. Interestingly, their siblings showed similarly reduced brain activation patterns although they did not have ASD. These similar patterns of decreased activity shared by ASD children and their unaffected siblings are called "trait markers." The researchers also identified other distinct brain regions that showed decreased activity only in the children with ASD, which they termed "state markers." Because these state markers are unique to ASD children, they could potentially serve as biomarkers for the disorder. Finally, the scientists identified brain regions in unaffected siblings that showed heightened levels of activity that they termed "compensatory regions." The increased activity in these regions may provide clues about why – with similar genetic risk – only one of the siblings developed ASD. The study gives insight into the brain basis of ASD and may help to improve diagnosis based on the newly identified neural signatures.

A Model for Neural Development and Treatment for Rett Syndrome Using Human Induced Pluripotent Stem Cells

Marchetto MC, Carromeu C, Acab A, Yu D, Yeo GW, Mu Y, Chen G, Gage FH, Muotri AR. Cell. 2010 Nov 12;143(4):527-39.

Researchers were able to create a neuronal model of Rett syndrome, a disorder on the autism spectrum with a known genetic cause, using induced pluripotent stem cells (iPSCs) from people with the disorder. Studying neurons produced from human Rett syndrome patients may help scientists gain a better understanding of the biological basis of Rett syndrome and be useful in testing potential drug interventions. This is the first time an iPSC model of ASD has been created. In the study, researchers collected skin cells from four female patients with Rett syndrome and five healthy controls. By introducing a retrovirus, the scientists were able to reprogram the cells to behave like embryonic stem cells – giving them the ability to become an assortment of different cell types. Using the iPSCs, the researchers created functional neurons that were identical in many ways to those found in mouse models of Rett syndrome and postmortem brain tissue from individuals with the disorder. The neurons created from the participants with Rett syndrome showed structural and functional defects when compared to the cells from healthy controls. They were found to have 50 percent fewer synapses, a reduced number of dendritic spines (which help to send cellular signals), and smaller cell bodies. The neurons also showed abnormalities in their signaling abilities. With additional tests, the researchers were able to show that the abnormalities seen in the neurons stemmed from the mutations in the gene MECP2 that causes Rett syndrome. With this knowledge, they were able to treat the neurons with several drugs, reversing the cell defects and restoring normal cell signaling. The effective drugs included insulin growth factor 1 (IGF-1), previously shown to restore function in mouse models of Rett, and the antibiotic gentamicin, which increased MeCP2 levels by suppressing a type of mutation that commonly causes Rett syndrome. The study suggests that drug therapies could be effective for children with Rett syndrome when used early in development, before symptoms arise at 6 to 18 months of age. The ability to create patient-specific cellular models of a neurodevelopmental disorder offers a powerful new tool for researchers studying potential drug treatments.

Longitudinal MRI Study of Cortical Development Through Early Childhood in Autism

Schumann CM, Bloss CS, Barnes CC, Wideman GM, Carper RA, Akshoomoff N, Pierce K, Hagler D, Schork N, Lord C, Courchesne E. J Neurosci. 2010 Mar 24;30(12):4419-27.

An imaging study conducted over several years confirmed what many researchers have long hypothesized – children with ASD experience a period of early brain overgrowth beginning at a very young age. While this hypothesis has been supported by studies of head circumference and cross-sectional magnetic resonance imaging (MRI) of the brain, it had not been confirmed through a longitudinal study of brain growth during the critical period when symptoms of ASD first arise. Using functional MRI, researchers collected brain scans from toddlers who were later diagnosed with ASD and their typically developing peers at several points between 1 1/2 years and 5 years of age. The study included 193 scans from 44 typically developing children and 41 children who went on to be diagnosed with ASD at around 4 years of age. The scans showed that by 21/2 years of age, the brain's two major components – white and gray matter – were significantly enlarged in toddlers with ASD when compared to their peers. The greatest amount of enlargement occurred in regions of the brain known as the frontal, temporal, and cingulate cortices. As the children with ASD aged, overgrowth was seen in almost all parts of the brain. There were significant differences between genders, with girls showing more dramatic overgrowth in more regions. This suggests that the abnormal brain development in males and females with ASD may be fundamentally different. Based on the results of this research, the authors recommend including younger children in future studies to determine when brain overgrowth begins. They also suggest considering genetic information and other biomarkers to better understand the underlying biological processes that affect the brain and result in the symptoms of ASD. As a caveat, the authors note that autism is a very heterogeneous disorder and not all children with ASD show brain enlargement. Future studies may help to identify the different patterns of neurodevelopment of individual subgroups.

Question 3: Risk Factors - What Caused This to Happen and Can It Be Prevented?

Mutations in the SHANK2 Synaptic Scaffolding Gene in Autism Spectrum Disorder and Mental Retardation

Berkel S, Marshall CR, Weiss B, Howe J, Roeth R, Moog U, Endris V, Roberts W, Szatmari P, Pinto D, Bonin M, Riess A, Engels H, Sprengel R, Scherer SW, Rappold GA. Nat Genet. 2010 Jun;42(6):489-91.

Researchers discovered that mutations to SHANK2, a gene believed to play a role in maintaining the inner structure of the synapse, were present in people with ASD, as well as those with intellectual impairment. Without proper structure at the postsynapse – the receiving end of cellular communication – neural impulses cannot be properly sent. A gene in the same family, SHANK3, has previously been linked with ASD. The researchers sequenced SHANK2 in 396 people with ASD, 184 people with mental retardation, and 659 typically developing individuals. They found instances of copy number variations (CNVs), submicroscopic deletions and insertions of DNA, in two people with ASD. The CNVs were de novo, meaning they had arisen spontaneously and were not inherited from a parent. Seven inherited changes in SHANK2 were also found in people with ASD or intellectual impairment – the fact that their parents were carriers of these variants but did not show signs of atypical development suggests that a certain threshold of mutation must be reached to result in a disorder. A single nonsense de novo mutation (a type of mutation that usually results in a nonfunctional protein product) was also found.

Overall, the study is notable because it identified additional examples of overlapping genes associated with both ASD (with and without cognitive impairment) and intellectual disability.

Blood Mercury Concentrations in CHARGE Study Children with and without Autism

Hertz-Picciotto I, Green PG, Delwiche L, Hansen R, Walker C, Pessah IN. Environ Health Perspect. 2010 Jan;118(1):161-6.

A study found that children with ASD have similar levels of mercury in their blood as typically developing children, after controlling for other factors that impact mercury levels.

The greatest predictor of blood mercury levels was the amount of fish in the child's diet.

Almost all fish contain a trace amount of mercury and some larger predatory fish like swordfish and tuna may contain high levels. (The study adjusted for the fact that children with ASD generally ate less fish than their peers.) Researchers measured mercury levels in three groups of children ranging from 2 to 5 years of age: those with ASD, those with another developmental disorder, and those developing typically. The children were all enrolled in a study investigating factors that may contribute to ASD called the Childhood Autism Risk from Genetics and Environment (CHARGE) study. The children's mothers were interviewed to determine ways in which the child could have been exposed to mercury, including fish consumption, personal care products like nasal sprays that may contain mercury, and silver-colored mercury-based amalgam fillings. Vaccine information was collected from the children's medical records and was not found to have any association with blood mercury levels. Overall, children with ASD had similar blood mercury levels to that of the general population. Children with developmental disabilities other than ASD consistently showed lower levels than the other groups.

Apart from fish consumption, tooth-grinding and gum-chewing with mercury-based amalgam fillings was also linked to higher mercury levels. The authors caution that the study did not investigate whether mercury exposure in either prenatal or early postnatal period plays a role in causing ASD because blood measures were taken from children who had already been diagnosed with the disorder.

Functional Impact of Global Rare Copy Number Variation in Autism Spectrum Disorder

Pinto D, Pagnamenta AT, Klei L, Anney R, Merico D, Regan R, Conroy J, Magalhaes TR, Correia C, Abrahams BS, Almeida J, Bacchelli E, Bader GD, Bailey AJ, Baird G, Battaglia A, Berney T, Bolshakova N, Bölte S, Bolton PF, Bourgeron T, Brennan S, Brian J, Bryson SE, Carson AR, Casallo G, Casey J, Chung BH, Cochrane L, Corsello C, Crawford EL, Crossett A, Cytrynbaum C, et al. Nature. 2010 Jul 15;466(7304):368- 72.

Researchers studying the genetics of ASD have identified a set of rare genetic variations that may confer risk for the disorder. While ASD is known to have a strong genetic component, (studies of identical twins have shown a 90 percent likelihood that both siblings are affected, compared to a 10 percent rate for non-identical twins), the exact genetic causes of ASD are still under investigation.

All known genetic causes of ASD account for only 5 to 15 percent of cases, leaving the majority unexplained. Previous studies have implicated mutations in several genes that relate to proper functioning at the synapse, the junction between neurons where cell signaling takes place, and other genes involved in neural development. In the study, researchers conducted in-depth genetic analyses to compare the genomes of 996 people with ASD to 1,287 typically developing individuals. They found that people with ASD had 19 percent more rare copy number variations (CNVs) – abnormalities in the number of copies of one or more sections of DNA. When taken individually, each CNV was found in less than 1 percent of people with ASD. These CNVs were most likely to occur in genes that had previously been linked to ASD and/or intellectual disability. By further investigating the genes where the majority of the CNVs occurred in people with ASD, the researchers identified four genes that had never before been associated with ASD. These genes, as well as others implicated in previous studies, seem to be involved in similar biochemical pathways in the brain – those involved in cognitive development or cell signaling and communication. The authors are hopeful that better understanding of pathways linked to ASD will eventually lead to targets for pharmaceutical treatments.

Altered Functional Connectivity in Frontal Lobe Circuits Is Associated with Variation in the Autism Risk Gene CNTNAP2

Scott-Van Zeeland AA, Abrahams BS, Alvarez-Retuerto AI, Sonnenblick LI, Rudie JD, Ghahremani D, Mumford JA, Poldrack RA, Dapretto M, Geschwind DH, Bookheimer SY. Sci Transl Med. 2010 Nov 3;2(56)56ra80.

Researchers have found that certain forms of the autism risk gene CNTNAP2 are linked to wiring issues in the brain that could explain problems with language acquisition and learning associated with the disorder. Using functional imaging scans to capture brain activity during a learning task, the researchers discovered that children with the risk gene had too many connections within the frontal lobe, the portion of the brain involved in learning and other higher-level mental functions, and too few connections between the frontal lobe and other parts of the brain. Long-range connections to the back of the brain were particularly weakened. Investigators looked at two variations of CNTNAP2 – one which conferred risk for ASD and another common variant of the gene which did not. In addition to connectivity issues between the front and the back of the brain, children with the risk gene also showed atypical connection patterns between the right and left hemispheres. Those without the risk gene generally had communication pathways in the frontal lobe that connected more strongly to the left side of the brain. Alternatively, children with the risk gene showed equal distribution between right and left hemispheres, suggesting that the variant rearranges the brain's circuitry and could interfere with language skills. Children with the risk gene showed these abnormal activation patterns regardless of whether they were diagnosed with ASD.

The findings suggest that CNTNAP2 plays an important role in wiring neurons in the frontal lobe and that mutations to the gene could disturb this process. This theory builds on earlier findings showing that CNTNAP2 is most active during development of the frontal lobe. In the future, understanding how genes can affect brain function and behavior could improve ASD diagnosis and potentially lead to interventions that aim to strengthen necessary connections within the brain. The finding may also apply to other disorders associated with CNTNAP2 variants, including speech and language impairments, attention deficit hyperactivity disorder (ADHD), Tourette syndrome, and schizophrenia.

Question 4: Interventions - Which Treatments and Interventions Will Help?

Randomized, Controlled Trial of an Intervention for Toddlers with Autism: The Early Start Denver Model

Dawson G, Rogers S, Munson J, Smith M, Winter J, Greenson J, Donaldson A, Varley J. Pediatrics. 2010 Jan;125(1):e17-23.

The Early Start Denver Model (ESDM) is the first comprehensive behavioral intervention for ASD shown to be effective for toddlers. This model uses a relationship-based approach that draws on elements of Applied Behavior Analysis (ABA) – a style of therapy that emphasizes breaking activities into small, measurable units that are then reinforced with reward. In this study, researchers performed a randomized, controlled trial of the intervention over two years and showed that it led to improvements in IQ, language abilities, and adaptive functioning (i.e., the skills necessary for everyday activities). It also reduced the overall severity of ASD, with a substantial proportion of the children changing from a diagnosis of autism to a milder classification of Pervasive Developmental Disability, Not Otherwise Specified (PDD-NOS). During the study, 48 toddlers diagnosed with ASD, 1'A to 2'A years of age, were randomly assigned to receive the Early Start Denver Model or an intervention commonly available in the community. Children in the Early Start Denver Model group received an average of 15 hours per week working one-on-one with a therapist trained in the technique. Parents were taught to continue the therapy at home for at least 5 hours a week.

The other 24 toddlers worked with therapists in the area, receiving a range of conventional therapies, for an average of 9 hours a week and received an additional 9 hours of therapy in a specialized preschool or other group program. Overall, the average number of intervention hours was similar between the two groups.

After two years, the children receiving the Early Start Denver Model intervention showed a 17.6 point increase in IQ compared to a 7 point increase in the comparison group working with community therapists. The children in the Early Start Denver Model group also showed continued growth in adaptive behaviors (e.g., brushing teeth, getting dressed, eating with utensils, etc.), while the other children fell further behind their typically developing peers. Notably, 7 of the 24 children in the Early Start Denver Model group had significant enough improvements to change from a diagnosis of ASD to PDD-NOS. Only one of the children in the comparison group had a change in diagnosis. This study is the first randomized, controlled trial of an intervention for toddlers with ASD and adds to the body of evidence supporting the importance of early diagnosis and treatment.

Randomized Controlled Caregiver Mediated Joint Engagement Intervention for Toddlers with Autism

Kasari C, Gulsrud AC, Wong C, Kwon S, Locke J. J Autism Dev Disord. 2010 Sep;40(9):1045-56.

A study found that a parent-led intervention for toddlers with autism improved the children's responsiveness to joint engagement and increased the variety of their play. Joint attention skills involve the ability to engage others using eye contact or gestures to communicate nonverbally (e.g., pointing to a toy, looking between an event and a parent to share interest). Research has shown that children with better joint attention skills go on to have better language skills, suggesting that teaching joint engagement may be an important focus of early ASD interventions. During the study, parents were trained to lead 24 therapy sessions over 8 weeks. The interventions incorporated aspects of Applied Behavior Analysis (ABA) and focused on following the child's lead in activities and maintaining his interest. Parents were taught to engage his or her child by imitating his actions, talking about what the child was doing, repeating back and expanding on things the child said, and making eye contact throughout the session. Researchers assessed how strictly parents adhered to the treatment principles and how comfortably they led the session. After completing the parent-led intervention, the 19 toddlers showed that they had successfully moved from play that was primarily object-focused to play with increased levels of joint engagement. However, the intervention only improved the children's responsiveness to joint engagement initiated by the parent and did not improve the children's own ability to initiate joint engagement. While the study showed that most of the parents strictly adhered to the treatment protocol, the level of fidelity did not predict how well his or her child responded to the intervention. The quality of the parent's interaction during the session also did not affect outcome, nor did the type or amount of additional treatment the child was receiving. Notably, the study is one of the first to show that a parent-mediated intervention can improve joint attention skills and diversity of play. The authors note that it will be important to gauge how the effectiveness of parent-mediated interventions compares to those led by therapists.

Evaluation of Comprehensive Treatment Models for Individuals with Autism Spectrum Disorders

Odom SL, Boyd BA, Hall LJ, Hume K. J Autism Dev Disord. 2010 Apr;40(4):425-36.

A study evaluated 30 treatment models for ASD, assessing whether the procedures were well-documented, how many times the model had been replicated, and how much evidence existed to support the effectiveness of the model's interventions. Overall, the study found that the procedures for using the models, most of which were based on aspects of Applied Behavior

Analysis, were well-documented in manuals or guides. However, few of the models had developed measures to assess whether the model was well-implemented. Most of the models had been replicated by others – almost half had been repeated two or more times at independent sites. The weakest aspect was proof of effectiveness – 16 of the 30 models had never published research on their effectiveness in a peer-reviewed journal. The authors evaluated the models using journal articles, book chapters, web pages, procedural manuals, and phone interviews with the models' developers. After assessing the evidence, the researchers found that five models scored highly on at least four of the six dimensions that were evaluated: the Denver Model, LEAP (Learning Experiences and Alternative Programs for Preschoolers and Their Parents), Lovaas Institute, May Institute, and PCDI (Princeton Child Development Institute). Models with low evaluation scores included the following: Hanen, Higashi, Eden, Summit, Lancaster, and Son Rise. These rankings can be used as a guide for researchers, service providers, and families faced with treatment decisions. In the future, model developers will need to create measures to verify that the model has been effectively implemented. Additional research will also be necessary to document that the interventions are effective.

Evidence-Based Practices in Interventions for Children and Youth with Autism Spectrum Disorders

Odom S, Collet-Klingenberg L, Rogers SJ, Hatton DD. Preventing School Failure. 2010;54(4):275-82.

Investigators reviewed the research literature to identify educational techniques for students with ASD that have sufficient evidence to support their effectiveness. While education programs are expected to be built upon evidence-based practices, currently there are no guidelines to identify whether an intervention is adequately supported by research. After developing a set of criteria, the researchers identified 24 intervention practices that qualify as "evidence-based." The study evaluated individual instructional practices or strategies (e.g., social skills training groups, positive behavioral support strategies, etc.), rather than comprehensive treatment models like the Denver Model or Lovaas Model. For studies to be considered as evidence of the practice's effectiveness, they had to include children with ASD younger than 22 years of age, measure outcome, show that gains in a targeted area clearly followed the use of the practice, and have sufficient controls for comparison. The practice needed support from at least two experimental studies (subjects are randomly assigned to groups) or observational studies (subjects are not randomly assigned but researchers can draw inferences about the effect of the treatment from the data) carried out by independent researchers. Practices that could only be supported by single-subject design – where subjects function as their own control group – would be deemed evidence-based only if there were at least five studies from three independent research groups. (A combination of several single-subject design and experimental/observational studies was also allowed.) After identifying the list of evidence-based practices, the researchers developed a chart matching the practice with the improved skill areas (academic, behavior, communication, play, social, and transitions). Practitioners and families can use the chart to identify which evidence-based practice has been shown effective in the skill area related to the student's learning objectives. The team also constructed web-based modules that include implementation instructions and procedural guidelines for each of the practices. The authors note that the number of evidence-based practices is expected to grow as more literature on ASD interventions is published.

Question 5: Services - Where Can I Turn for Services?

Can State Early Intervention Programs Meet the Increased Demand of Children Suspected of Having Autism Spectrum Disorders?

Wise MD, Little AA, Holliman JB, Wise PH, Wang CJ. J Dev Behav Pediatr. 2010 Jul-Aug;31(6):469-76.

Early Intervention programs may be strained by the increase in demand for ASD services and additional resources will likely be necessary, according to reports from state program coordinators. In 2007, the American Academy of Pediatrics recommended that all children be screened for ASD at 18 and 24 months of age. Since that time, most states have seen a greater demand for ASD evaluations and behavioral services. The Early Intervention program provides ASD services for many young children (less than 36 months of age) across the United States, including almost all lower-income children on the spectrum. While the program is funded through the Individuals with Disabilities Education Act (IDEA), each state is expected to coordinate its own program and as a result services vary across states. Widespread staff shortages have made meeting the additional demand for services difficult, with almost half of the Early Intervention coordinators reporting that children in their state or territory receive 5 hours or fewer of weekly services. Only four states reported that most children receive more than 20 hours a week, indicating that the majority of children in Early Intervention programs are not receiving the 25 hours of behavioral intervention recommended by the National Research

Council. Reports of personnel shortages were common, with 89 percent of coordinators reporting a need for behavioral therapists, 82 percent reporting a need for speech-language pathologists, and 79 percent for occupational therapists. Staff shortages were more likely to occur in states with a greater percentage of African-American and Latino children. Almost half of states reported that these personnel shortages pose a challenge to creating Individualized Family Services Plans (IFSPs), which guide the early intervention process for children with disabilities and their families, within the required 45-day time limit. Notably, several of the coordinators commented that the intensity of the plans should be scrutinized as well – many programs will only include services in IFSPs that can realistically be provided in the state, rather than the optimal course of treatment (e.g., calling for 5 hours of behavioral therapy when 25 would be ideal). The authors conclude that more resources will be needed to meet the increased demand for services as a result of enhanced early screening. Dedication to strengthening local services will be particularly important during a time when budget pressure could result in deep cuts to available services.

Question 6: Lifespan - What Does the Future Hold, Particularly for Adults?

While no articles.directly related to Question 6: *What does the future hold, particularly for adult?* were selected by the committee for inclusion in the final *2010 IACC Summary of Advances in Autism Spectrum Disorder Research* , three articles were nominated in this category and they are listed on page 24 of this document in the Full Listing of Nominated Articles.

Question 7: Infrastructure - What Other Infrastructure and Surveillance Needs Must Be Met?

Changes in Autism Spectrum Disorder Prevalence in 4 Areas of the United States

Rice C, Nicholas J, Baio J, Pettygrove S, Lee LC, Van Naarden Braun K, Doernberg N, Cunniff C, Newschaffer C, Meaney FJ, Charles J, Washington A, King L, Kolotos M, Mancilla K, Ervis CA, Carpenter L, Yeargin-Allsopp M. Disability and Health Journal. July 2010;3(3):186-201.

Researchers analyzed changes in the rates of ASD in four states from 2000 to 2004 and found that the prevalence had increased by an average of 55 percent in the locations showing change. Using data collected by the Centers for Disease Control and Prevention (CDC) Autism and Developmental Disabilities Monitoring (ADDM) Network, researchers found that prevalence rates had increased significantly in Georgia and Maryland (38 percent and 72 percent increases respectively).

In Arizona, rates of ASD increased by 26 percent over the four years, but this figure did not rise to the level of statistical significance (meaning that the measured increase could have occurred by chance and may not represent the true prevalence change). In South Carolina, ASD rates dropped, but not by a statistically significant amount, effectively representing no change in prevalence. Investigators identified 8-year-olds who met the DSM-IV criteria for ASD by reviewing information about their development included in their available health and/or education records.

The authors note that some of the increase in prevalence is due to heightened awareness, change in diagnostic criteria, earlier age of diagnosis, and the diagnosis of milder forms of ASD; however, taken together, these factors do not entirely explain the increase in prevalence and a true surge in the number of cases cannot be ruled out. Regardless of the cause, there is a dramatic change in the prevalence of ASD in some parts of the country, and more children are accessing services than ever before. In the face of such an urgent public health concern, the authors state that collaborative efforts to improve research and service systems for people with ASD will be essential, in addition to continued monitoring to better understand changes in prevalence.

Full Listing of Nominated Articles

Question 1: When Should I Be Concerned?

Chowdhury M, Aman MG, Scahill L, Swiezy N, Arnold LE, Lecavalier L, Johnson C, Handen B, Stigler K, Bearss K, Sukhodolsky D, McDougle CJ. The Home Situations Questionnaire-PDD version: factor structure and psychometric properties. *J. Intellect. Disabil. Res.* 2010 Mar;54(3):281-91.

King TM, Tandon SD, Macias MM, Healy JA, Duncan PM, Swigonski NL, Skipper SM, Lipkin PH. Implementing developmental screening and referrals: lessons learned from a national project. *Pediatrics.* 2010 Feb;125(2):350-60.

Mandell DS, Morales KH, Xie M, Lawer LJ, Stahmer AC, Marcus SC. Age of diagnosis among Medicaid-enrolled children with autism, 2001-2004. *Psychiatr. Serv.* 2010 Aug;61(8):822-9.

Miller DT, Adam MP, Aradhya S, Biesecker LG, Brothman AR, Carter NP, Church DM, Crolla JA, Eichler EE, Epstein CJ, Faucett WA, Feuk L, Friedman JM, Hamosh A, Jackson L, Kaminsky EB, Kok K, Krantz ID, Kuhn RM, Lee C, Ostell JM, Rosenberg C, Scherer SW, Spinner NB, Stavropoulos DJ, Tepperberg JH, Thorland EC, Vermeesch JR, Waggoner DJ, Watson MS, Martin CL, Ledbetter DH. Consensus statement: Chromosomal microarray is a first-tier clinical diagnostic test for individuals with developmental disabilities or congenital anomalies. *Am. J. Hum. Genet.* 2010 May 14;86(5):749-64.

Norris M, Lecavalier L. Screening accuracy of Level 2 autism spectrum disorder rating scales: A review of selected instruments. *Autism. 2010 Jul;14(4):263-84.*

Oller DK, Niyogi P, Gray S, Richards JA, Gilkerson J, Xu D, Yapanel U, Warren SF. Automated vocal analysis of naturalistic recordings from children with autism, language delay, and typical development. *Proc. Natl. Acad. Sci. USA*. 2010 Jul. 27;107(30):13354-9.

Ozonoff S, Iosif AM, Baguio F, Cook IC, Hill MM, Hutman T, Rogers SJ, Rozga A, Sangha S, Sigman M, Steinfeld MB, Young GS. A prospective study of the emergence of early behavioral signs of autism. *J. Am. Acad. Child Adolesc. Psychiatry.* 2010 Mar;49(3):256-66.e1-2.

Question 2: How Can I Understand What Is Happening?

Buie T, Campbell DB, Fuchs, III GJ, Furuta GT, Levy J, Van de Water J, Whitaker AH, Atkins D, Bauman ML, Beaudet AL, Carr EG, Gershon MD, Hyman SL, Jirapinyo P, Jyonouchi H, Kooros K, Kushak R, Levitt P, Levy SE, Lewis JD, Murray KF, Natowicz MR, Sabra A, Wershil BK, Weston SC, Zeltzer L, Winter H. Evaluation, diagnosis, and treatment of gastrointestinal disorders in individuals with ASDs: a consensus report. *Pediatrics.* 2010 Jan; 125: S1 - S18.

Buie T, Fuchs GJ 3rd, Furuta GT, Kooros K, Levy J, Lewis JD, Wershil BK, Winter H. Recommendations for evaluation and treatment of common gastrointestinal problems in children with ASDs. *Pediatrics*. 2010 Jan;125(Suppl 1):S19-29.

Chamberlain SJ, Chen PF, Ng KY, Bourgois-Rocha F, Lemtiri-Chlieh F, Levine ES, Lalande M. Induced pluripotent stem cell models of the genomic imprinting disorders Angelman and Prader-Willi syndromes. *Proc. Natl. Acad. Sci. USA*. 2010 Oct 12;107(41):17668-73.

Chao HR, Chen H, Samaco RC, Xue M, Chahrour M, Yoo J, Neul JL, Gong S, Lu HC, Heintz N, Ekker M, Rubenstein JL, Noebels JL, Rosenmund C, Zoghbi HY. Dysfunction in GABA signaling mediates autism-like stereotypies and rett syndrome phenotypes. *Nature*. 2010 Nov 11;468(7321):263-9.

Ecker C, Marquand A, Mourao-Miranda J, Johnston P, Daly EM, Brammer MJ, Maltezos S, Murphy CM, Robertson D, Williams SC, Murphy DG. Describing the brain in autism in five dimensions— magnetic resonance imaging-assisted diagnosis of autism spectrum disorder using a multiparameter classification approach. *J. Neurosci.* 2010 Aug11; 30(32):10612-23.

Giulivi C, Zhang YF, Omanska-Klusek A, Ross-Inta C, Wong S, Hertz-Picciotto I, Tassone F, Pessah IN. Mitochondrial dysfunction in autism. *JAMA*. 2010 Dec. 1;304(21):2389-96.

Kaiser MD, Hudac CM, Shultz S, Lee SM, Cheung C, Berken AM, Deen B, Pitskel NB, Sugrue DR, Voos AC, Saulnier CA, Ventola P, Wolf JM, Klin A, Vander Wyk BC, Pelphrey KA. Neural signatures of autism. *Proc. Natl. Acad. Sci. USA*. 2010 Dec 7;107(49):21223-8.

Marchetto MC, Carromeu C, Acab A, Yu D, Yeo GW, Mu Y, Chen G, Gage FH, Muotri AR. A model for neural development and treatment of Rett syndrome using human induced pluripotent stem cells. *Cell*. 2010 Nov 12;143(4):527-39.

Mostafa GA, El-Hadidi ES, Hewedi DH, Abdou MM. Oxidative stress in Egyptian children with autism: relation to autoimmunity. *J. Neuroimmun.* 2010 Feb. 26;219(1-2):114-8.

Palmieri L, Papaleo V, Porcelli V, Scarcia P, Gaita L, Sacco R, Hager J, Rousseau F, Curatolo P, Manzi B, Militerni R, Bravaccio C, Trillo S, Schneider C, Melmed R, Elia M, Lenti C, Saccani M, Pascucci T, Puglisi-Allegra S, Reichelt KL, Persico AM. Altered calcium homeostasis in autism-spectrum disorders: evidence from biochemical and genetic studies of the mitochondrial aspartate/glutamate carrier AGC1. *Mol. Psychiatry*. 2010 Jan;15(1):38-52.

Palmieri L, Persico AM. Mitochondrial dysfunction in autism spectrum disorders: Cause or effect? *Biochim. Biophys. Acta.* 2010 June - July;1797(6-7):1130-1137.

Schumann CM, Bloss CS, Barnes CC, Wideman GM, Carper RA, Akshoomoff N, Pierce K, Hagler D, Schork N, Lord C, Courchesne E. Longitudinal magnetic resonance imaging study of cortical development through early childhood in autism. *J. Neurosci.* 2010 Mar 24;30(12):4419-27.

Zikopoulos B, Barbas H. Changes in prefrontal axons may disrupt the network in autism. *J. Neurosci.* 2010 Nov 3;30(44):14595-609.

Question 3: What Caused This to Happen and Can It Be Prevented?

Berkel S, Marshall CR, Weiss B, Howe J, Roeth R, Moog U, Endris V, Roberts W, Szatmari P, Pinto D, Bonin M, Riess A, Engels H, Sprengel R, Scherer SW, Rappold GA. Mutations in the SHANK2 synaptic scaffolding gene in autism spectrum disorder and mental retardation. *Nat. Genet.* 2010 Jun;42(6):489-91.

Campbell DB, Warren D, Sutcliffe JS, Lee EB, Levitt P. Association of MET with social and communication phenotypes in individuals with autism spectrum disorder. *Am. J. Med. Genet. B Neuropsychiatr. Genet.* 2010 Mar 5;153B(2):438-46.

Curtis JT, Hood AN, Chen Y, Cobb GP, Wallace DR. Chronic metals ingestion by prairie voles produces sex-specific deficits in social behavior: an animal model of autism. *Behav Brain Res.* 2010 Nov 12;213(1):42-9.

Gallagher CM, Goodman MS. Hepatitis B vaccination of male neonates and autism diagnosis, NHIS 1997- 2002. *J. Toxicol. Environ. Health A.* 2010;73(24):1665-77.

Girirajan S, Rosenfeld JA, Cooper GM, Antonacci F, Siswara P, Itsara A, Vives L, Walsh T, McCarthy SE, Baker C, Mefford HC, Kidd JM, Browning SR, Browning BL, Dickel DE, Levy DL, Ballif BC, Platky K, Farber DM, Gowans GC, Wetherbee JJ, Asamoah A, Weaver DD, Mark PR, Dickerson J, Garg BP, Ellingwood SA, Smith R, Banks VC, Smith W, McDonald MT, Hoo JJ, French BN, Hudson C, Johnson JP, Ozmore JR, Moeschler JB, Surti U, Escobar LF, El-Khechen D, Gorski JL, Kussmann J, Salbert B, Lacassie Y, Biser A, McDonald-McGinn DM, Zackai EH, Deardorff MA, Shaikh TH, Haan E, Friend KL, Fichera M, Romano C, Gécz J, DeLisi LE, Sebat J, King

MC, Shaffer LG, Eichler EE. A recurrent 16p12.1 microdeletion supports a two-hit model for severe developmental delay. *Nat. Genet.* 2010 Mar;42(3):203-9.

Hertz-Picciotto I, Green PG, Delwiche L, Hansen R, Walker C, Pessah IN. Blood mercury concentrations in CHARGE Study children with and without autism. *Environ. Health Perspect.* 2010 Jan;118(1):161- 6.

Hunter JW, Mullen GP, McManus JR, Heatherly JM, Duke A, Rand JB. Neuroligin-deficient mutants of C. elegans have sensory processing deficits and are hypersensitive to oxidative stress and mercury toxicity. *Dis. Model. Mech.* 2010 May-Jun;3(5-6):366-76.

Johnson S, Hollis C, Kochhar P, Hennessy E, Wolke D, Marlow N. Autism spectrum disorders in extremely preterm children. *J. Pediatr.* 2010 Apr.;156(4):525-31.e2.

Keil A, Daniels JL, Forssen U, Hultman C, Cnattingius S, Söderberg KC, Feychting M, Sparen P. Parental autoimmune diseases associated with autism spectrum disorders in offspring. *Epidemiology.* 2010 Nov;21(6):805-8.

Kern JK, Geier DA, Adams JB, Geier MR. A biomarker of mercury body-burden correlated with diagnostic domain specific clinical symptoms of autism spectrum disorder. *Biometals*. 2010 Dec;23(6):1043-1051.

Lancet. Retraction--Ileal-lymphoid-nodular hyperplasia, non-specific colitis, and pervasive developmental disorder in children. *Lancet.* 2010 Feb 6;375(9713):445.

Lichtenstein P, Carlstrom E, Rastam M, Gillberg C, Anckarsater H. The genetics of autism spectrum disorders and related neuropsychiatric disorders in childhood. *Am. J. Psychiatry.* 2010 Nov;167(11):1357-63.

Lintas C, Altieri L, Lombardi F, Sacco R, Persico AM. Association of autism with polyomavirus infection in postmortem brains. *J. Neurovirol.* 2010 Apr;16(2):141-9.

Olczak M, Duszczyk M, Mierzejewski P, Wierzba-Bobrowicz T, Majewska MD. Lasting neuropathological changes in rat brain after intermittent neonatal administration of thimerosal. *Folia Neuropathol.* 2010;48(4):258-69.

Pinto D, Pagnamenta AT, Klei L, Anney R, Merico D, Regan R, Conroy J, Magalhaes TR, Correia C, Abrahams BS, Almeida J, Bacchelli E, Bader GD, Bailey AJ, Baird G, Battaglia A, Berney T, Bolshakova N, Bölte S, Bolton PF, Bourgeron T, Brennan S, Brian J, Bryson SE, Carson AR, Casallo G, Casey J, Chung BH, Cochrane L, Corsello C, Crawford EL, Crossett A, Cytrynbaum C, et al. Functional impact of global rare copy number variation in autism spectrum disorders. *Nature.* 2010 Jul. 15;466(7304):368-72.

Price CS, Thompson WW, Goodson B, Weintraub ES, Croen LA, Hinrichsen VL, Marcy M, Robertson A, Eriksen E, Lewis E, Bernal P, Shay D, Davis RL, DeStefano F. Prenatal and infant exposure to thimerosal from vaccines and immunoglobulins and risk of autism. *Pediatrics.* 2010 Oct;126(4):656-64.

Schieve LA, Baio J, Rice CE, Durkin M, Kirby RS, Drews-Botsch C, Miller LA, Nicholas JS, Cunniff CM. Risk for cognitive deficit in a population-based sample of U.S. children with autism spectrum disorders: Variation by perinatal health factors. *Disability and Health Journal.* July 2010; 3(3) 202-212.

Scott-van Zeeland AA, Abrahams BS, Alvarez-Retuerto AI, Sonnenblick LI, Rudie JD, Ghahremani D, Mumford JA, Poldrack RA, Dapretto M, Geschwind DH, Bookheimer SY. Altered functional connectivity in frontal lobe circuits is associated with variation in the autism risk gene CNTNAP2. *Sci. Transl. Med.* 2010 Nov 3;2(56)56ra80.

Shelton JF, Tancredit DJ, Hertz-Picciotto I. Independent and dependent contributions of advanced maternal and paternal ages to autism risk. *Autism Res. 2010 Feb;3(1):30-9.*

Shoffner J, Hyams L, Langley GN, Cossette S, Mylacraine L, Dale J, Ollis L, Kuoch S, Bennett K, Aliberti A, Hyland K. Fever plus mitochondrial disease could be risk factors for autistic regression. *J. Child Neurol.* 2010 Apr;25(4):429-34.

Smith MJ, Woods CR. On-time vaccine receipt in the first year does not adversely affect neuropsychological outcomes. *Pediatrics.* 2010 Jun;125(6):1134-41.

Yap IK, Angley M, Veselkov KA, Holmes E, Lindon JC, Nicholson JK. Urinary metabolic phenotyping differentiates children with autism from their unaffected siblings and age-matched controls. *J.Proteome. Res.* 2010 Jun 4;9(6):2996-3004.

Question 4: Which Treatments and Interventions Will Help?

Arnold LE, Farmer C, Kraemer HC, Davies M, Witwer A, Chuang S, DiSilvestro R, McDougle CJ, McCracken J, Vitiello B, Aman MG, Scahill L, Posey DJ, Swiezy NB. Moderators, mediators, and other predictors of risperidone response in children with autistic disorder and irritability. *J. Child Adolesc. Psychopharmacol.* 2010 Apr;20(2):83-93.

Dawson G, Rogers S, Munson J, Smith M, Winter J, Greenson J, Donaldson A, Varley J. Randomized, controlled trial of an intervention for toddlers with autism: The Early Start Denver Model. *Pediatrics.* 2010 Jan;125(1):e17-23.

Frankel F, Myatt R, Sugar C, Whitham C, Gorospe CM, Laugeson E. A randomized controlled study of parent-assisted Children's Friendship Training with children having autism spectrum disorders. *J. Autism Dev. Disord.* 2010 Jul;40(7):827-42.

Kasari C, Gulsrud AC, Wong C, Kwon S, Locke J. Randomized controlled caregiver mediated joint engagement intervention for toddlers with autism. *J. Autism Dev. Disord.* 2010 Sep;40(9):1045- 56.

McCracken JT, Aman MG, McDougle CJ, Tierney E, Shiraga S, Whelan F, Arnold LE, Posey D, Ritz L, Vitiello B, Scahill L. Possible influence of variant of the P-glycoprotein gene (MDR1/ABCB1) on clinical response to guanfacine in children with pervasive developmental disorders and hyperactivity. *J. Child Adolesc. Psychopharmacol.* 2010 Feb;20(1):1-5.

Odom S, Collet-Klingenberg L, Rogers SJ, Hatton DD. Evidence-based practices in interventions for children and youth with autism spectrum disorders. *Preventing School Failure.* 2010 May;54(4):275-82.

Odom SL, Boyd BA, Hall LJ, Hume K. Evaluation of comprehensive treatment models for individuals with autism spectrum disorders. *J. Autism Dev. Disord.* 2010 Apr;40(4):425-36.

Question 5: Where Can I Turn for Services?

Brookman-Frazee L, Taylor, R, Garland, A. Characterizing Community-Based Mental Health Services for Children with Autism Spectrum Disorders and Disruptive Behavior Problems. *J. Autism Dev. Disord.* 2010 Oct;40(10): 1188-1201.

Wehmeyer, MI, Shogren KA, Smith TEC, Zager D, Simpton R. Research-Based Principles and Practices for Educating Students with Autism: Self-Determination and Social Interactions. *Education and Training in Autism and Developmental Disabilities.* 2010 45(4): 475-86.

Young J, Corea C, Kimani J, Mandell D. Autism Spectrum Disorders (ASDs) Services: Final Report on Environmental Scan. *Prepared for the Centers for Medicare & Medicaid Services.* 2010 Mar 9.

Wise MD, Little AA, Holliman JB, Wise PH, Wang CJ. Can state early intervention programs meet the increased demand of children suspected of having autism spectrum disorders? *J. Dev. Behav. Pediatr.* 2010 Jul Aug;31(6):469-76.

Question 6: What Does the Future Hold, Particularly for Adults?

Chowdhury M, Benson BA, Hillier A. Changes in Restricted Repetitive Behaviors with age: A study of high-functioning adults with Autism Spectrum Disorders. *Research in Autism Spectrum Disorders.* 2010 April-June;4(2):210-216.

LeBel J, Huckshorn KA, Caldwell, B. Restraint use in residential programs: why are best practices ignored? *Child Welfare.*2010;89(2):169-87.

McDonough JT, Revell G. Accessing employment supports in the adult system for transitioning youth with autism spectrum disorders. *Journal of Vocational Rehabilitation.* 2010;32(2):89-100.

Question 7: What Other Infrastructure and Surveillance Needs Must Be Met?

Durkin MS, Maenner MJ, Meaney FJ, Levy SE, DiGuiseppi C, Nicholas JS, Kirby RS, Pinto-Martin JA, Schieve LA. Socioeconomic inequality in the prevalence of autism spectrum disorder: evidence from a U.S. cross-sectional study. *PLoS. One.* 2010 Jul 12;5(7):e11551.

Gilberg C, Billstedt E, Sundh V, Gilbert IC. Mortality in autism: a prospective longitudinal community-based study. *J. Autism Dev. Disord.* 2010 Mar;40 (3): 352-57.

Liu KY, King M, Bearman PS. Social influence and the autism epidemic. *AJS.* 2010 Mar;115(5):1387-434.

Mazumdar S, King M, Liu KY, Zerubavel N, Bearman P. The spatial structure of autism in California, 1993- 2001. *Health Place.* 2010 May;16(3):539-46.

McDonald ME, Paul JF. Timing of increased autistic disorder cumulative incidence. *Environ Sci Technol.* 2010 Mar 15;44(6):2112-8.

Rice C, Nicholas J, Baio J, Pettygrove S, Lee LC, Van Naarden Braun K, Doernberg N, Cunniff C, Newschaffer C, Meaney FJ, Charles J,

Washington A, King L, Kolotos M, Mancilla K, Ervis CA, Carpenter L, Yeargin-Allsopp M. Changes in autism spectrum disorder prevalence in 4 areas of the United States. *Disabil Health J.* July 2010;3(3):186-201.

Saemundsen E, Juliusson H, Hjaltested S, Gunnarsdottir T, Halldorsdottir T, Hreidarsson S, Magnusson P. Prevalence of autism in an urban population of adults with severe intellectual disabilities - a preliminary study. *J. Intellect Disabil. Res.* 2010 Aug;54(8):727-35.

van Meter KC, Christiansen LE, Delwiche LD, Azari R, Carpenter TE, Hertz-Picciotto I. Geographic distribution of autism in California: a retrospective birth cohort analysis. *Autism Res.* 2010 Feb;3(1):19-29.

In: Advances in Autism Spectrum Disorder ... ISBN: 978-1-62257-058-4
Editors: R. L. Jackson and A. C. Lee

Chapter 5

2011 Summary of Advances in Autism Spectrum Disorder Research*

The Interagency Autism Coordinating Committee

About the IACC

The Interagency Autism Coordinating Committee (IACC) is charged with providing advice to the Secretary of Health and Human Services (HHS) and with coordinating all efforts within HHS concerning autism spectrum disorder (ASD). It was established by Congress under the Combating Autism Act of 2006 and renewed under the Combating Autism Reauthorization Act of 2011.

Membership of the committee includes a wide array of federal agencies involved in ASD research and services, as well as public stakeholders who represent a variety of perspectives from within the autism community. This makeup of the IACC membership is designed to ensure that the committee is equipped to address the wide range of issues and challenges faced by families and individuals affected by autism.

Under the CAA, the IACC is required to (1) develop and annually update a Strategic Plan for ASD research, (2) develop and annually update a summary of advances in ASD research, and (3) monitor federal activities related to ASD.

---

* This is an edited, reformatted and augmented version of The Interagency Autism Coordinating Committee publication.

In completing these tasks, the members of the committee have worked collaboratively to advance biomedical research and coordinate services that will make an impact for people with ASD and their families. *For more information about the IACC, see www.iacc.hhs.gov.*

INTRODUCTION

Each year the IACC releases its annual list of scientific advances that represent significant progress in the field. The twenty studies selected have given new insight into the complex causes of autism and potential risk factors, studied clues that could lead to earlier diagnosis, and evaluated promising early intervention strategies. The advances also address the prevalence of ASD both in the U.S. and internationally, as well as the service needs of people with ASD across the lifespan. The 2011 Summary of Advances provides short, plain language synopses of the top research breakthroughs selected by the committee from a pool of peer-reviewed articles nominated by the members. Articles are grouped according to the questions of the IACC Strategic Plan for ASD Research (available at www.iacc.hhs.gov). Citations for the articles selected for the Summary of Advances, as well as a complete listing of those nominated, are included at the end of the document.

ARTICLES SELECTED FOR THE 2011 SUMMARY OF ADVANCES

Question 1: When Should I Be Concerned?

Disrupted Neural Synchronization in Toddlers with Autism

Dinstein I, Pierce K, Eyler L, Solso S, Malach R, Behrmann M, Courchesne E. Neuron. 2011 Jun 23;70(6):1218-25.

A study of sleeping toddlers identified patterns of abnormal neural activity that could aid in the early diagnosis of autism and help to understand underlying causes. Using functional magnetic resonance imaging (fMRI), researchers found that 72 percent of children with ASD showed decreased synchronization across brain hemispheres in areas commonly associated with language and communication. This decreased synchronization was rarely seen in typically developing children, or those with delayed language development who did not have autism. Strong synchronization between the right and left hemisphere of the brain is critical for proper functioning, and there is evidence of disrupted synchronization in neurological disorders such as schizophrenia and Alzheimer's disease. While disrupted synchronization has been documented in adults with autism, researchers had been unable to study the phenomenon in early childhood because toddlers cannot remain still long enough to undergo a brain scan when awake. Researchers were able to overcome this challenge by performing scans on sleeping children; neurons remain synchronized between regions of the brain with similar function even while resting. The brain scans revealed that weak neural synchronicity is evident in the early stages of autism and that the strength of synchronization is linked to the degree of the child's symptoms -- children with the weakest neural synchronization exhibit the most severe impairments. The researchers note that measures of neural synchronization could one day play a role in early autism diagnosis, particularly because the measure can be taken while the child sleeps.

Detecting, Studying, And Treating Autism Early: The One-Year Well-Baby Check-Up Approach

Pierce K, Carter C, Weinfeld M, Desmond J, Hazin R, Bjork R, Gallagher N. J Pediatr. 2011 Sep;159(3):458- 465.e1-6.

A five-minute checklist filled out by parents at the one-year, well-baby check-up has been shown to predict autism or other developmental delays in about 75 percent of cases. This easily implemented tool is the first validated autism screen for infants and could help pediatricians identify autism even earlier than the evaluations at 18 and 24 months of age recommended by the American Academy of Pediatrics. The screening tool, called the *Communication and Symbolic Behavior Scales Developmental Profile Infant-Toddler Checklist*, developed by Dr. Amy Wetherby and colleagues, was filled out by parents in the waiting room and took pediatricians only two minutes to review, providing a quick way to identify young children at risk for ASD. The study followed 137 pediatricians in San Diego County who used the tool to screen almost 10,500 infants. About 12 percent of infants screened were flagged by the questionnaire as at-risk for ASD and referred for further evaluation at a clinic. The study followed 184 infants who failed the screen until three years of age and found that 17 percent (32 children) ultimately received an autism diagnosis. Of the remaining children, 30 percent were identified as having a learning disability, 5 percent with a developmental disability, and 20 percent as another type of disability. Overall, the screen yielded about a 30 percent false-positive rate, meaning that 1 out of 3 infants flagged as at-risk during the initial screen did not subsequently receive a developmental disorder diagnosis. The findings demonstrate that the checklist is a convenient and effective screen for autism and other disabilities at the one-year, well-baby check-up – improving the chances of early detection and increasing the opportunity for early intervention. Notably, all 137 pediatricians who participated in the study were still using the checklist when the article was published -- a significant improvement from the only 22 percent who were screening at one-year check-ups prior to the study.

Question 2: How Can I Understand What Is Happening?

Mutations Causing Syndromic Autism Define an Axis of Synaptic Pathophysiology

Auerbach BD, Osterweil EK, Bear MF. Nature. 2011 Nov 23;480(7375): 63-8.

New research reveals that two genetic forms of autism, fragile X syndrome and tuberous sclerosis, are actually caused by opposite malfunctions – while fragile X is caused by overproduction of proteins at the synapse, tuberous sclerosis is caused by underproduction. Interestingly, while the causes of fragile X and tuberous sclerosis are distinctly different, both disorders often result in intellectual disability and autism spectrum disorder. Researchers made the discovery while studying mGluR5 (Metabotropic glutamate receptor 5), a receptor on the surface of neurons that is key in aiding communication at the synapse – the junction between neurons. During normal signaling, the mGluR5 receptor binds to the neurotransmitter glutamate after it is released across the synapse, resulting in the production of new synaptic proteins. Fragile X protein (FMRP) halts protein synthesis to ensure that the appropriate amount is produced -- in fragile X syndrome, changes to the gene that controls FMRP allow synaptic proteins to continue production unchecked, resulting in too much protein. Researchers have previously shown that introducing a substance to block mGluR5 reverses some of the symptoms of fragile X, and human drug trials are currently underway. Armed with an understanding of the underlying causes of fragile X, researchers in this study examined mice with tuberous sclerosis mutations and discovered something surprising. In this case, the disorder was caused by the opposite malfunction – too little protein synthesis at the synapse, which could be treated with a drug stimulating mGluR5. Further, when the researchers bred the two mice together, many of their autistic features went away. The findings of the study indicate that proper brain function can only occur within a narrow range of mGluR5 protein synthesis – changes in either direction lead to syndromes with similar behavioral symptoms. This also suggests that drug treatments for autism spectrum disorder will need to be individually tailored, as conditions that appear similar may have quite different underlying causes.

Absence of CNTNAP2 Leads to Epilepsy, Neuronal Migration Abnormalities, and Core Autism-Related Deficits

Peñagarikano O, Abrahams BS, Herman EI, Winden KD, Gdalyahu A, Dong H, Sonnenblick LI, Gruver R, Almajano J, Bragin A, Golshani P, Trachtenberg JT, Peles E, Geschwind DH. Cell. 2011 Sep 30;147(1):235-46.

A new mouse model of autism, created by eliminating a gene strongly associated with the disorder in humans, shows promise for understanding the biology that underlies ASD and testing new treatments. By eliminating the CNTNAP2 gene (contactin associated protein-like 2), researchers were able to create mice with behaviors that closely mimicked those of its human counterparts – the mice exhibited repetitive behaviors, abnormal social interactions, and irregular vocalizations, in addition to experiencing seizures and hyperactivity.CNTNAP2 is thought to play an important role in the development of language, and variants of the gene have been linked to an increased risk of autism and epilepsy. Prior to experiencing seizures, the mice showed signs of abnormal brain circuit development – researchers observed irregularities in communication between neurons and their migration within the brain.

These observations complement earlier studies suggesting that children with autism carrying a CNTNAP2 variant have a "disjointed brain." The frontal lobe is poorly connected with the rest of the brain but shows an overconnection with itself, resulting in poor communication with other brain regions.

Notably, the mice in the study responded positively to risperidone, an antipsychotic medication approved by the FDA to treat symptoms of irritability and aggression associated with ASD.

While their social interactions did not improve – risperidone has not been shown to improve social function in humans – there was a marked improvement in repetitive grooming and a decrease in hyperactivity. Creating an animal model of autism that closely resembles the symptoms and behaviors in humans may be an important tool in understanding neural development in autism and developing new treatments.

Protein Interactome Reveals Converging Molecular Pathways

Sakai Y, Shaw CA, Dawson BC, Dugas DV, Al-Mohtaseb Z, Hill DE, Zoghbi HY. Sci. Transl. Med. 2011 Jun 8;3(86):86ra49.

A recent study sheds light on how a variety of different mutations in genes that seemingly have little in common can each result in the symptoms of autism. To answer this question, researchers developed a molecular map of protein networks or "interactome" to identify how proteins associated with ASD interact with hundreds of other proteins. Researchers used genes known to be associated with syndromic autism as a starting point for building the interactome. Syndromic autism occurs as part of a broader genetic disorder such as fragile X, Angelman syndrome, and Rett syndrome -- understanding protein interactions with syndromic autism may give insight into idiopathic autism, or autism with no known cause. Using 26 genes associated with syndromic autism, researchers hypothesized that the seemingly dissimilar genes might interact with shared partners in common molecular pathways, leading to the symptoms of autism. Indeed, researchers identified a complex network of 539 proteins that interacted with the autism-related proteins, successfully demonstrating that all of the proteins linked to autism are connected by interactions with common partners. The interactome confirmed previously suspected gene relationships and several new pairings, such as the connection between SHANK3 and TSC1, which share 21 common protein partners. Researchers then performed a microarray analysis on 288 individuals with idiopathic autism in a search for genes within the interactome. They identified three novel copy number variations -- chromosomal deletions and duplications -- on genes found in the network, demonstrating that the interactome may help to identify new genes related to ASD and understand complicated genetic variation.

Transcriptomic Analysis of Autistic Brain Reveals Convergent Molecular Pathways

Voineagu I, Wang X, Johnston P, Lowe JK, Tian Y, Horvath S, Mill J, Cantor RM, Blencowe BJ, Geschwind DH. Nature. 2011 May 25;474 (7351):380-4.

A study found surprising consistency in molecular changes seen in the brains of people with autism across the spectrum, suggesting a common biological basis that may span multiple subtypes. Researchers analyzed postmortem brain tissue and found atypical patterns of gene expression common to many of the individuals with ASD. These findings may provide clues about how autism changes the brain at the molecular level, and lead to new avenues for developing treatments. In the study researchers focused on gene expression -- the way information from the gene is used in the synthesis of functional gene products, often proteins. These proteins then perform specific tasks in the cell. In brains affected by autism, genes involved in neuron function and communication were expressed at much lower levels than in typically developing individuals, and the expression of genes involved in certain immune functions was abnormally high. The authors note that many of these genes are active during fetal development, supporting the theory that abnormal brain development may start very early in the womb. The findings also provide evidence that molecular changes in neuron function and communication are probably a cause of autism, rather than a result of the disorder. To identify common patterns of gene expression among people with autism, the researchers compared the frontal and temporal lobes of the brain – the frontal lobe is responsible for higher-level thinking including judgment and social response, while the temporal lobe plays a key role in hearing and language and is also involved in sensory integration. They found that more than 500 genes were expressed at different levels in the frontal and temporal lobes of typically developing individuals, as would be expected in separate brain regions with differing functions. However, there was almost no difference in the levels of gene expression between the two regions in the brains of those with ASD. This blurring suggests a failure to differentiate regions in early brain development.

Question 3: What Caused This to Happen and Can It Be Prevented?

Genetic Heritability and Shared Environmental Factors Among Twin Pairs with Autism

Hallmayer J, Cleveland S, Torres A, Phillips J, Cohen B, Torigoe T, Miller J, Fedele A, Collins J, Smith K, Lotspeich L, Croen LA, Ozonoff S, Lajonchere C, Grether JK, Risch N. Arch Gen Psychiatry. 2011 Nov;68(11):1095-102.

Recent research suggests that environmental factors may play a much greater role in autism risk than previously suspected and could even be more influential than genetic factors. These findings stem from a study of autism in twins, the largest of its kind, designed to model the genetic and environmental factors that contribute to the development of autism. Because identical twins share 100 percent of their DNA, researchers can assess the degree to which a disorder is genetic by studying the number of cases where both twins are affected (called concordance). Fraternal twins share 50 percent of their DNA, similar to siblings, so by comparing concordance rates among fraternal twins and siblings, researchers can study the influence of environmental factors, particularly those in the womb. In the study, researchers looked at concordance among 192 pairs of identical and fraternal twins and found that 77 percent of male identical twins and 50 percent of female twins were both affected by autism. Previous studies with smaller numbers of twins suggested a much greater genetic contribution, as high as 90 percent. The fraternal twins in the study had a 35 percent concordance rate – much lower than rates among identical twins but higher than rates among siblings, estimated to range from 3 to 19 percent. Using mathematical modeling, the researchers propose that environmental factors accounted for 55 percent of autism risk, while genetic heritability contributed less than 40 percent. The difference in rates among fraternal twins and siblings, who share similar amounts of DNA, suggests that environmental factors in the womb may be an important area of future study.

Rare De Novo and Transmitted Copy-Number Variation in Autistic Spectrum Disorders

Levy D, Ronemus M, Yamrom B, Lee YH, Leotta A, Kendall J, Marks S, Lakshmi B, Pai D, Ye K, Buja A, Krieger A, Yoon S, Troge J, Rodgers L, Iossifov I, Wigler M. Neuron. 2011 Jun 9;70(5):886-97.

A study of the genetic causes of autism confirmed that spontaneous or *de novo* mutations are present in a substantial number of families with only one child on the spectrum. These *de novo* mutations are not inherited from parents' DNA, arising instead in their egg or sperm or very early in embryonic development. Researchers compared the DNA of children with ASD to that of their unaffected sibling(s) and identified a diverse array of rare genetic abnormalities that may contribute to autism. Recent advances in technology have allowed researchers to identify genetic mutations on a finer scale than was previously possible. Some of the *de novo* mutations, known as copy number variations (CNVs) because they contain deleted or duplicated sections of DNA, were located in regions known to be associated with ASD, while others implicate new regions. Many of the mutations are thought to affect genes or gene networks involved in brain development. The study confirmed that these non-inherited CNVs are more common in children with ASD compared to their non-affected siblings; however, each unique variant is exceedingly rare, some found in only one family. In addition, researchers found evidence that inherited "ultrarare" genetic duplications may also contribute to autism. Based on the results of the study, the authors note that females have a greater resistance to autism from genetic causes, raising questions about the fate of female carriers. The study findings emphasize the diversity of rare genetic variations that contribute to ASD and suggest the possibility that a treatment for one form of autism may not have value for the majority of cases. The DNA samples analyzed in the study were part of the Simons Simplex Collection, a repository of over 1,000 families in the U.S. and Canada with only one child on the spectrum.

Exome Sequencing In Sporadic Autism Spectrum Disorders Identifies Severe De Novo Mutations

O'Roak BJ, Deriziotis P, Lee C, Vives L, Schwartz JJ, Girirajan S, Karakoc E, Mackenzie AP, Ng SB, Baker C, Rieder MJ, Nickerson DA, Bernier R, Fisher SE, Shendure J, Eichler EE. Nat Genet. 2011 Jun;43(6):585-9.

Another study of spontaneous mutations identified four genes that are likely to play a causal role in the development of autism. Instead of searching more broadly for copy number variants throughout the genome, researchers focused exclusively on the protein-coding region of the genome called the exome. This approach has a greater potential to identify single candidate genes for ASD. The study sequenced the exomes of 20 people with autism and their parents and identified 21 spontaneous or *de novo* mutations. Of the 21 mutations, four were determined to be potentially causative (FOXP1, GRIN2B, SCN1A, and LAMC3). Of note, the four participants carrying these mutations were profoundly affected by autism. Three of the four genes identified in the study had previously been associated with autism, intellectual disability without autism, and epilepsy. The fourth mutation, LAMC3, had never before been linked to autism and represents a potential new avenue of research. Within the study, two of the four children had been hit with a "genetic double-whammy" – both inheriting a harmful gene mutation from his parent and having a *de novo* mutation. For example, the child with a FOXP1 mutation also inherited a defective copy of CNTNAP2, believed to be involved in language development. This child had severe autism and the most profound language deficits of any participant. Another child with autism and epilepsy had both an inherited deletion putting him at risk for epilepsy and a *de novo* mutation of a gene associated with epilepsy, SCN1A. These two cases support the 'multi-hit' theory of autism – that a combination of mutations in the same pathway is necessary to cause severe autism or related disorders. The authors note that the study supports the role of *de novo* mutations as a major genetic contributor to autism and demonstrates the great potential of whole exome sequencing to identify candidate genes.

Recurrence Risk for Autism Spectrum Disorders: A Baby Siblings Research Consortium Study

Ozonoff S, Young GS, Carter A, Messinger D, Yirmiya N, Zwaigenbaum L, Bryson S, Carver LJ, Constantino JN, Dobkins K, Hutman T, Iverson JM, Landa R, Rogers SJ, Sigman M, Stone WL. Pediatrics. 2011 Sep; 128 (3) e488-95.

For parents with an autistic child, the risk of having another child with autism may be greater than previously thought, according to findings from the largest prospective study of baby siblings conducted to date. Earlier studies suggested that 3 to 10 percent of infants who had an older sibling with autism would go on to develop the disorder themselves – new findings suggest that the risk of recurrence is substantially higher, at approximately 19 percent. This risk is even greater if the younger sibling is a boy or if he or she has more than one older sibling with ASD – male siblings have a 1 in 4 chance of developing autism while those from multiplex families have almost a 1 in 3 chance. Other factors, such as the severity of symptoms in the older sibling, older sibling's gender, parental age, or birth order were not shown to have any effect on recurrence risk. In this study, researchers recruited 664 infants and tracked them from around 8 months of age to 36 months when they were tested for autism. Ultimately, 132 children were diagnosed with autism spectrum disorder using gold-standard direct assessment methods. The research was conducted through the Baby Siblings Research Consortium, an international network that pools data to learn more about children at high risk for developing autism. The researchers note that the increased risk of autism recurrence for siblings suggests that families and pediatricians should take special care tracking their development and refer them for early intervention should concerns arise. These findings also have important implications for genetic counseling and family planning purposes.

Multiple Recurrent De Novo Cnvs, Including Duplications of the 7q11.23 Williams Syndrome Region, Are Strongly Associated with Autism

Sanders SJ, Ercan-Sencicek AG, Hus V, Luo R, Murtha MT, Moreno-De-Luca D, Chu SH, Moreau MP, Gupta AR, Thomson SA, Mason CE, Bilguvar K, Celestino-Soper PB, Choi M, Crawford EL, Davis L, Davis Wright NR, Dhodapkar RM, Dicola M, Dilullo NM, Fernandez TV, Fielding-Singh V,

Fishman DO, Frahm S, Garagaloyan R, Goh GS,Kammela S, Klei L, Lowe JK, Lund SC, McGrew AD, Meyer KA, Moffat WJ, Murdoch JD, O'Roak BJ, Ober GT, Pottenger RS, Raubeson MJ, Song Y, Wang Q, Yaspan BL, Yu TW, Yurkiewicz IR, Beaudet AL, Cantor RM, Curland M, Grice DE, Günel M, Lifton RP, Mane SM, Martin DM, Shaw CA, Sheldon M, Tischfield JA, Walsh CA, Morrow EM, Ledbetter DH, Fombonne E, Lord C, Martin CL, Brooks AI, Sutcliffe JS, Cook EH Jr, Geschwind D, Roeder K, Devlin B, State MW. Neuron. 2011 Jun 9;70(5):863-85.

A recent collaborative study identified six genetic mutations that are strongly associated with autism spectrum disorder, including an area of DNA that likely holds clues to understanding the nature of human social behavior. The researchers estimate that these mutations represent only a few of the hundreds of spontaneously arising variants that are likely to increase autism risk. Using gene chip or microarray technology, the researchers analyzed the genomes of over 1,100 families with a single child on the autism spectrum, and compared the results of affected and unaffected siblings. The DNA samples analyzed in the study were part of the Simons Simplex Collection. The scan revealed a variety of copy number variants (CNVs) -- genetic mutations that can range from micro-deletions and duplications to large sequences of missing or additional DNA. Notably, one of the non-inherited or de novo CNVs was located on a genetic region linked to Williams-Beuren syndrome, a rare disorder that causes people to be extremely social, overly trusting, and highly empathetic. While loss of DNA from the area results in Williams-Beuren syndrome, gain of extra DNA in this area is associated with autism, which is marked by difficulty with social interaction and lack of empathy. This region’s connection with both disorders suggests its importance in understanding the nature of the social brain. The study also supports earlier findings of higher rates of de novo CNVs in people with autism compared to their unaffected siblings. Uncovering the genetic basis of autism is critical to understanding the neurobiology underlying the disorder and may aid in developing targeted treatment approaches for different subtypes.

Question 4: Which Treatments and Interventions Will Help?

A Systematic Review of Medical Treatments for Children with Autism Spectrum Disorders

McPheeters ML, Warren Z, Sathe N, Bruzek JL, Krishnaswami S, Jerome RN, Veenstra-Vanderweele J. Pediatrics. 2011 May;127(5):e1312-21.

Researchers conducted a systematic literature review to evaluate the effectiveness of drug treatments for children with autism spectrum disorder, age 12 and younger. While there was strikingly little evidence to support the benefits of most medications prescribed for children with ASD, the antipsychotics risperidone and aripiprazole showed clear benefit for managing challenging and repetitive behavior. Both drugs had at least one randomized controlled trial, considered the gold standard for intervention studies, conducted by the pharmaceutical company that produces each drug and at least two randomized controlled trials showing parent-reported benefits. The strength of the evidence for aripiprazole was considered to be high, while risperidone was deemed moderate. Despite benefits, both drugs cause significant side effects including marked weight gain, sedation, and a number of movement disorders; as a result, they are generally limited to patients with severe impairment or risk of injury. The systematic review also examined antidepressants and stimulants and found insufficient evidence to evaluate the effectiveness of either type of drug in reducing challenging and repetitive behavior in children with ASD. A widespread search across multiple databases identified only one good-quality and one fair-quality randomized controlled trial of serotonin reuptake inhibitors (SRIs) and one good-quality randomized controlled trial of stimulants. Study quality was determined by two reviewers who independently assessed the studies based on factors such as study design, participant characterization, diagnostic approach, outcome measurement, and statistical analysis. The authors note the need for more publicly funded studies to evaluate the potential benefits and risks of medications currently being prescribed for children on the spectrum.

Intervention Targeting Development of Socially Synchronous Engagement in Toddlers with Autism Spectrum Disorder: A Randomized Controlled Trial

Landa RJ, Holman KC, O'Neill AH, Stuart EA. J Child Psychol Psychiatry. 2011 Jan;52(1):13-21.

Two-year-olds with ASD showed improved social skills after completing an intervention targeting core social deficits in autism. It is the first randomized controlled trial to test such an intervention in toddlers and gives promise that a supplementary curriculum could improve social and communication skills in very young children. The researchers randomly assigned 50 toddlers with ASD, aged 21 to 33 months, to receive either an intervention called Interpersonal Synchrony - which targets social imitation, joint attention skills, and sharing of emotions - or a comparison intervention that does not target these specific social skills. Both six-month interventions were used for 10 hours per week in the classroom, and parents in both groups were given similar levels of training to continue the intervention at home. While toddlers in both groups showed gains in social, cognitive, and language skills during the study, children who received the Interpersonal Synchrony intervention, which encouraged them to communicate and play with others, had the greatest progress. At the end of the six months, these children had more than doubled the instances in which they engaged in social imitation (such as imitating the way a parent plays with a toy or mimicking a facial expression), while also making eye contact. Social imitation is believed to be critical in developing social communication skills -- deficits in such core social skills are a defining characteristic of autism. Importantly, children in the Interpersonal Synchrony group were able to generalize their newly developed skills to new people and settings. While their progress slowed in the six months following the end of the intervention, they did not lose any of the skills gained, unlike children in the comparison group who showed poorer social communication skills at the six-month follow-up.

Randomized, Controlled Trial of The LEAP Model of Early Intervention for Young Children with Autism Spectrum Disorders

Strain PS and Bovey EH. Topics in Early Childhood Special Education. 2011 Nov;31(3):133-154.

A 2011 study supports the effectiveness of an early intervention model for autism spectrum disorder designed to be used in an integrated classroom. Randomized controlled trials are considered to be the gold standard of evidence; however, due to their complexity and cost, only four other RCTs of comprehensive interventions for young children with autism had been completed at the time this article was published. Of these four, all were tested in segregated environments and involved one-on-one instruction at the beginning of the intervention. In contrast, the LEAP (Learning Experiences and Alternative Program for Preschoolers and Their Parents) preschool model uses teaching opportunities that arise naturally in an integrated setting and incorporates typically developing students by training them to support the social skills development of their peers with ASD. The LEAP model is also the first evidence-based intervention for ASD to be tested in a public school setting. In the study, researchers compared the performance of students in 28 classrooms where teachers received personal training and coaching support in the LEAP model over two years to the performance of teachers in 28 classrooms who received only training manuals and written materials. While all children had equivalent skill levels at the start of the intervention, after two years the students in the coached classrooms showed marked improvement in symptoms of autism, cognitive scores, language development, social skills, and a reduction in problem behavior. The teachers' fidelity to the LEAP strategies predicted the students' level of improvement. These findings suggest that successfully adhering to LEAP strategies produces broad developmental improvements. It costs much less than other commonly used one-on-one strategies -- an estimated $20,000 per child annually compared to $45,000 - $69,000.

Question 5: Where Can I Turn for Services?

Post-High School Service Use Among Young Adults with an Autism Spectrum Disorder

Shattuck PT, Wagner M, Narendorf S, Sterzing P, Hensley M. Arch Pediatr Adolesc Med. 2011 Feb;165(2):141-6.

A study of service use among young adults with autism showed a dramatic decline in the use of services after leaving high school. Use of medical, mental health, and case management services decreased, with nearly two-fifths (39%) of young adults reportedly receiving no services at all. The loss of school-based services comes at a critical juncture when young adults with autism may be transitioning into a new living situation, forming new types of relationships, or adjusting to the demands of work or vocational training. Researchers analyzed data about service use provided by 410 families of young adults with ASD, 19 to 23 years of age, who had recently left high school. This information was compared to data collected from most of the families six years earlier. While in school, 46 percent of the adolescents received mental health services, 47 percent received medical services, and 64 percent had a case manager. Six years later, these figures fell to 35 percent receiving mental health services, 24 percent receiving medical services, and 42 percent with a case manager. The greatest decline was seen in speech therapy, with a drop from 75 percent to 9 percent in the years following high school. Race and socioeconomic status played a strong role in predicting levels of service engagement, with African-American youths more than three times as likely to become completely disengaged after leaving school compared to white youths. Young adults from families making less than $25,000 annually were almost six times more likely to be disengaged than those from more affluent families making $75,000 a year or more. The authors note that these disparities indicate a need for targeted outreach and services.

Question 6: What Does the Future Hold, Particularly for Adults?

Epidemiology of Autism Spectrum Disorders in Adults in the Community In England

Brugha TS, McManus S, Bankart J, Scott F, Purdon S, Smith J, Bettington P, Jenkins R, Meltzer H. Arch Gen Psychiatry. 2011 May;68(5):459-65.

Approximately 1 percent of adults in England have autism spectrum disorder, based on one of the first studies of adult prevalence in the country. Previous studies have relied primarily on self-report which can be unreliable. To determine what proportion of the English population age 16 years and older is affected by autism, researchers conducted a multiphase study to screen adults in the community. They hypothesized that the rate of autism would be much lower in older adults than in children and that adults on the spectrum would be predominately male and socially disadvantaged. In the first phase of the study, participants selected from the 2007 Adult Psychiatric Morbidity Survey in England completed the Autism-Spectrum Quotient self-questionnaire. The answers to this and other self-assessments helped the investigators select 618 individuals from the initial 7,461 respondents to interview using the Autism Diagnostic Observation Schedule (ADOS-4). Based on the results of screening using the tool, 19 people met the criteria for autism spectrum disorder representing a prevalence rate of 9.8 per 1,000 individuals, or nearly 1 percent. While only a small number of individuals were identified, many were living in social housing and had the lowest levels of education, reinforcing the authors' hypothesis that those with autism are more likely to be socially disadvantaged. None of these associations, however, were statistically significant. The authors note that the prevalence rate identified in this study is similar to the rate reported among children, supporting the idea that autism rates have not changed significantly over time. Due to the small sample of adults with ASD, they were unable to examine differences in adult prevalence by age. The findings suggest that adults with ASD may be undiagnosed and socially disadvantaged, which has significant public health implications.

Autism Spectrum Disorders in Older Adults: Toward Defining a Research Agenda

Piven J, Rabins P; Autism-in-Older Adults Working Group. J Am Geriatr Soc. 2011 Nov;59(11):2151-55.

Relatively little is known about older adults with autism spectrum disorder – few studies have been done to determine how behaviors and symptoms change over time, how aging may impact people with ASD differently, and whether findings in children and young adults with ASD generalize to the older adult population. Based on current estimates, by 2030 there will be approximately 700,000 adults with ASD over the age of 65. Much work must be done to identify the unique service needs of this group and ensure that adequate long-term care options exist. To address the lack of knowledge about older adults with ASD, a multidisciplinary group convened in March 2010 to begin defining a research agenda to address the needs of the population. The group defined six research priorities, the first of which was the need for diagnostic criteria and instruments to identify individuals based on adult symptom profiles. Based on findings from a recent study in England, rates of autism appear to be relatively similar across generations suggesting that there is a large group of older adults with ASD who have gone undiagnosed.

Second, the group noted the need for studies characterizing symptoms, behaviors, and co-occurring conditions in adults, as well as available services and supports. Other priorities include the need for longitudinal research to study lifespan trajectories, neurobiological research to study how the autistic brain ages, and studies of different types of interventions for use with older adults on the spectrum. Finally, the group indentified the need to support training that would attract young researchers and clinicians to the emerging field of aging and autism. These proposed priorities should begin to answer questions about autism and aging in an effort to address individual needs and gauge its potential impact on the healthcare system and society.

Emerging New Practices in Technology to Support Independent Community Access for People with Intellectual and Cognitive Disabilities

Stock SE, Davies DK, Wehmeyer ML, Lachapelle Y. NeuroRehabilitation. 2011; 28(3):261-9.

New technology holds promise for helping people with cognitive disabilities access their community. A recent paper describes the various electronic devices and software applications currently on the market to help individuals navigate their community on foot and by public transit. While being unable to navigate one's community without assistance is a major barrier to community inclusion, little research has been devoted to exploring technologies that could promote community access. The authors review some of the advantages and drawbacks of emerging technologies for community access, and report results from a case study of a smartphone application in use. Of the technologies discussed, computer based video instruction (CBVI) has shown promise in small trials. Using CBVI, individuals are able to rehearse their routes using video shot from a first-person perspective while a voice-over gives instructions such as "push the request for stop signal when you see the Target sign." A three- person trial of CBVI found that two of the three participants were able to successfully generalize the skills they had rehearsed while on a public bus. Global Positioning System (GPS) technology used together with pictures of landmarks and audio cues has also been shown to be effective -- 24 out of 26 participants successfully traveled to a new destination unaccompanied using the system. A case study of a 19-yearold man with Down syndrome documented his use of a similar smartphone application to complete routes to four new destinations. Both he and his parents were extremely positive about the technology. In addition to enhancing self-determination and community integration, enabling people with cognitive disabilities to use public transit offers cost-savings. For example, a mid-size city would save more than $4,500 annually for each individual with cognitive disabilities who took a standard bus rather than specialized para-transit services.

Question 7: What Other Infrastructure and Surveillance Needs Must Be Met?

Trends in The Prevalence of Developmental Disabilities in US Children 1997-2008

Boyle C, Boulet S, Schieve LA, Cohen RA, Blumberg SJ, Yeagrin-Allsopp M, Visser S, Kogan MD. Pediatrics. 2011 Jun;127(6): 1034-42.

Developmental disorders among children in the U.S. increased in prevalence by 17.1 percent from 1997 to 2008, affecting an estimated 1.8 million more children than a decade before. Of all developmental disorders, autism showed the most growth, increasing 289 percent over the twelve-year time frame. During the same period, attention deficit hyperactivity disorder (ADHD) increased by 33 percent, while moderate to profound hearing loss, the only developmental disability to show improvement, decreased by 30.9 percent. In total, 15 percent of all children in the U.S. had some sort of developmental disability when last measured in 2008. Boys were more likely than girls to have a developmental disability and Hispanic children had a lower prevalence than other racial groups. The prevalence of developmental disabilities increased in all groups regardless of race or socio-economic status. Children from low-income families were more likely to have a developmental disability and those on Medicaid were nearly twice as likely to have a diagnosis. The study, conducted by the Centers for Disease Control and Prevention, analyzes data from 119,367 children ages 3 to 17 collected during National Health Survey Interviews. Parents or legal guardians were asked if their children had any of the following conditions: ADHD, autism, blindness, cerebral palsy, moderate to profound hearing loss, intellectual disability, learning disorders, seizures, stuttering/stammering, or any other developmental delay. The study authors conclude that the increased prevalence of developmental disorders demonstrated by the study underscores the heightened need for targeted health, education, and social services.

Prevalence of Autism Spectrum Disorders in a Total Population Sample

Kim YS, Leventhal BL, Koh YJ, Fombonne E, Laska E, Lim EC, Cheon KA, Kim SJ, Kim YK, Lee H, Song DH, Grinker RR. Am. J .Psychiatry. 2011 Sep;168(9):904-12.

A comprehensive study of school children in a region of South Korea revealed that approximately 1 in 38 children, or 2.6 percent, are on the autism spectrum. This study was the first of its kind to use total population sampling, and the findings suggest that using this technique might increase prevalence estimates in other countries. Researchers assessed more than 55,000 children between the ages of 5 and 12 living in the middle-class city of Goyang and found that two-thirds of the students with ASD were undiagnosed and had never received services. Only one third of the students with ASD were in the study's "high probability group" of 294 children enrolled in special education or listed on a disability registry. The rest of the children diagnosed with ASD were among the general population enrolled in mainstream classrooms. The authors note that if only the high probability group had been used to calculate prevalence, they would have arrived at a 0.7 percent prevalence rate -- similar to the 0.9 percent in the United States. They hypothesize that the low level of awareness about autism and the high degree of stigma surrounding the disorder in South Korea could partially explain the large number of undiagnosed children. To identify autism among children enrolled in mainstream classrooms, researchers asked parents and teachers to complete a 27-item questionnaire – children who screened positive for autism on the assessment were individually evaluated using gold-standard diagnostic methods.

The study findings suggest that total population studies may be necessary to produce more accurate ASD prevalence estimates. Further work will need to be done to determine whether the South Korean findings can be generalized to other countries.

Full Listing of Nominated Articles

Question 1: When Should I Be Concerned?

Bosl W, Tierney A, Tager-Flusberg H, Nelson C. EEG complexity as a biomarker for autism spectrum disorder risk. *BMC Med.* 2011 Feb 22;9:18.

Constantino JN. The quantitative nature of autistic social impairment. *Pediatr. Res.* 2011 May;69(5 Pt 2):55R-62R.

Dinstein I, Pierce K, Eyler L, Solso S, Malach R, Behrmann M, Courchesne E. Disrupted neural synchronization in toddlers with autism. *Neuron.* 2011 Jun 23;70(6):1218-25.

Libertus K, Needham A. Reaching experience increases face preference in 3-month-old infants. *Dev .Sci.* 2011 Nov;14(6):1355-64.

Mattila ML, Kielinen M, Linna SL, Jussila K, Ebeling H, Bloigu R, Joseph RM, Moilanen I. Autism spectrum disorders according to DSM-IV-TR and comparison with DSM-5 draft criteria: an epidemiological study. *J Am. Acad .Child Adolesc. Psychiatry.* 2011 Jun;50(6):583-592.e11.

Miller JS, Gabrielsen T, Villalobos M, Alleman R, Wahmhoff N, Carbone PS, Segura B. The each child study: systematic screening for autism spectrum disorders in a pediatric setting. *Pediatrics.* 2011 May;127(5):866-71.

Pierce K, Carter C, Weinfeld M, Desmond J, Hazin R, Bjork R, Gallagher N. Detecting, studying, and treating autism early: the one-year well-baby check-up approach. *J Pediatr.* 2011 Sep;159(3):458-465.e1-6.

Sasson NJ, Elison JT, Turner-Brown LM, Dichter GS, Bodfish JW. Brief report: circumscribed attention in young children with autism. *J. Autism. Dev. Disord.* 2011 Feb;41(2):242-7.

Question 2: How Can I Understand What Is Happening?

Auerbach BD, Osterweil EK, Bear MF. Mutations causing syndromic autism define an axis of synaptic pathophysiology. *Nature.* 2011 Nov 23;480(7375):63-8.

Bangash MA, Park JM, Melnikova T, Wang D, Jeon SK, Lee D, Syeda S, Kim J,Kouser M, Schwartz J, Cui Y, Zhao X, Speed HE, Kee SE, Tu JC, Hu JH, Petralia RS, Linden DJ, Powell CM, Savonenko A, Xiao B, Worley PF. Enhanced polyubiquitination of Shank3 and NMDA receptor in a mouse model of autism. *Cell.* 2011 May 27;145(5):758-72.

Cohen S, Gabel HW, Hemberg M, Hutchinson AN, Sadacca LA, Ebert DH, Harmin DA, Greenberg RS, Verdine VK, Zhou Z, Wetsel WC, West AE, Greenberg ME. Genome-wide activity-dependent MeCP2 phosphorylation regulates nervous system development and function. *Neuron.* 2011 Oct 6;72(1):72-85.

Courchesne E, Mouton PR, Calhoun ME, Semendeferi K, Ahrens-Barbeau C, Hallet MJ, Barnes CC, Pierce K. Neuron number and size in prefrontal cortex of children with autism. *JAMA.* 2011 Nov 9;306(18):2001-10.

Goldman S, McGrew S, Johnson K, Richdale A, Clemons T, Malow B. Sleep is associated with problem behaviors in children and adolescents with autism spectrum disorders. *Res. Autism Spectr. Disord.* Jul-Sep 2011;5(3):1223-29.

Peça J, Feliciano C, Ting JT, Wang W, Wells MF, Venkatraman TN, Lascola CD, Fu Z, Feng G. Shank3 mutant mice display autistic-like behaviours and striatal dysfunction. *Nature.* 2011 Apr 28;472(7344):437-42.

Peñagarikano O, Abrahams BS, Herman EI, Winden KD, Gdalyahu A, Dong H, Sonnenblick LI, Gruver R, Almajano J, Bragin A, Golshani P, Trachtenberg JT, Peles E, Geschwind DH. Absence of CNTNAP2 leads to epilepsy, neuronal migration abnormalities, and core autism-related deficits. *Cell.* 2011 Sep 30;147(1):235-46.

Sakai Y, Shaw CA, Dawson BC, Dugas DV, Al-Mohtaseb Z, Hill DE, Zoghbi HY. Protein interactome reveals converging molecular pathways among autism disorders. *Sci. Transl. Med.* 2011 Jun 8;3(86):86ra49.

Shriberg LD, Paul R, Black LM, van Santen JP. The hypothesis of apraxia of speech in children with autism spectrum disorder. *J. Autism. Dev. Disord.* 2011 Apr;41(4):405-26.

Voineagu I, Wang X, Johnston P, Lowe JK, Tian Y, Horvath S, Mill J, Cantor RM, Blencowe BJ, Geschwind DH. Transcriptomic analysis of autistic brain reveals convergent molecular pathology. *Nature*. 2011 May 25;474(7351):380-4.

Question 3: What Caused This to Happen and Can It Be Prevented?

Adams JB, Audhva T, McDonough-Means S, Rubin RA, Quig D, Geis E, Gehn E, Lorest M, Mitchell J, Atwood S, Barnhouse S, Lee W. Nutritional and metabolic status of children with autism vs. neurotypical children, and the association with autism severity. *Nutr. Metab. (Lond)*. 2011 Jun 8;8(1):34.

Adams JB, Johansen LJ, Powell LD, Quig D, Rubin RA. Gastrointestinal flora and gastrointestinal status in children with autism--comparisons to typical children and correlation with autism severity. *BMC Gastroenterol.* 2011 Mar 16;11:22.

Alter MD, Kharkar R, Ramsey KE, Craig DW, Melmed RD, Grebe TA, Bay RC, Ober-Reynolds S, Kirwan J, Jones JJ, Turner JB, Hen R, Stephan DA. Autism and increased paternal age related changes in global levels of gene expression regulation. *PLoS One.* 2011 Feb 17;6(2):e16715.

Ashwood P, Krakowiak P, Hertz-Picciotto I, Hansen R, Pessah I, Van de Water J. Elevated plasma cytokines in autism spectrum disorders provide evidence of immune dysfunction and are associated with impaired behavioral outcome. *Brain Behav. Immun.* 2011 Jan;25(1):40-5.

Blanchard KS, Palmer RF, Stein Z. The value of ecologic studies: mercury concentration in ambient air and the risk of autism. *Rev. Environ. Health.* 2011;26(2):111-8.

Bowers K, Li Q, Bressler J, Avramopoulos D, Newschaffer C, Fallin MD. Glutathione pathway gene variation and risk of autism spectrum disorders. *J. Neurodev. Disord.* 2011 Jun;3(2):132-43.

Delong G. A positive association found between autism prevalence and childhood vaccination uptake across the U.S. population. *J. Toxicol. Environ. Health A.* 2011 Jan;74(14):903-16.

Gardener H, Spiegelman D, Buka SL. Perinatal and neonatal risk factors for autism: a comprehensive meta-analysis. *Pediatrics.* 2011 Aug;128(2):344-55.

Garrecht M, Austin DW. The plausibility of a role for mercury in the etiology of autism: a cellular perspective. *Toxicol. Environ. Chem.* 2011 May;93(5-6):1251-1273.

Gilman SR, Iossifov I, Levy D, Ronemus M, Wigler M, Vitkup D. Rare *de novo* variants associated with autism implicate a large functional network of genes involved in formation and function of synapses. *Neuron.* 2011 Jun 9;70(5):898-907.

Goines PE, Croen LA, Braunschweig D, Yoshida CK, Grether J, Hansen R, Kharrazi M, Ashwood P, Van de Water J. Increased midgestational IFN-y, IL-4 and IL-5 in women bearing a child with autism: a case-control study. *Mol. Autism.* 2011 Aug 2;2:13.

Goines P, Haapanen L, Boyce R, Duncanson P, Braunschweig D, Delwiche L, Hansen R, Hertz-Picciotto I, Ashwood P, Van de Water J. Autoantibodies to cerebellum in children with autism associate with behavior. *Brain Behav. Immun.* 2011 Mar;25(3):514-23.

Hallmayer J, Cleveland S, Torres A, Phillips J, Cohen B, Torigoe T, Miller J, Fedele A, Collins J, Smith K, Lotspeich L, Croen LA, Ozonoff S, Lajonchere C, Grether JK, Risch N. Genetic heritability and shared environmental factors among twin pairs with autism. *Arch. Gen. Psychiatry.* 2011 Nov;68(11):1095-102.

Levy D, Ronemus M, Yamrom B, Lee YH, Leotta A, Kendall J, Marks S, Lakshmi B, Pai D, Ye K, Buja A, Krieger A, Yoon S, Troge J, Rodgers L, Iossifov I, Wigler M. Rare *de novo* and transmitted copy-number variation in autistic spectrum disorders. *Neuron.* 2011 Jun 9;70(5):886-97.

O'Roak BJ, Deriziotis P, Lee C, Vives L, Schwartz JJ, Girirajan S, Karakoc E, Mackenzie AP, Ng SB, Baker C, Rieder MJ, Nickerson DA, Bernier R, Fisher SE, Shendure J, Eichler EE. Exome sequencing in sporadic autism spectrum disorders identifies severe de novo mutations. *Nat. Genet.* 2011 Jun;43(6):585-9.

Ozonoff S, Young GS, Carter A, Messinger D, Yirmiya N, Zwaigenbaum L, Bryson S, Carver LJ, Constantino JN, Dobkins K, Hutman T, Iverson JM, Landa R, Rogers SJ, Sigman M, Stone WL. Recurrence risk for autism spectrum disorders: a Baby Siblings Research Consortium study. *Pediatrics.* 2011 Sep; 128(3):e488-95.

Sanders SJ, Ercan-Sencicek AG, Hus V, Luo R, Murtha MT, Moreno-De-Luca D, Chu SH, Moreau MP, Gupta AR, Thomson SA, Mason CE, Bilguvar K, Celestino-Soper PB, Choi M, Crawford EL, Davis L, Davis Wright NR, Dhodapkar RM, Dicola M, Dilullo NM, Fernandez TV, Fielding-Singh V, Fishman DO, Frahm S, Garagaloyan R, Goh GS,Kammela S, Klei L, Lowe JK, Lund SC, McGrew AD, Meyer KA, Moffat WJ, Murdoch JD, O'Roak BJ, Ober GT, Pottenger RS, Raubeson MJ, Song Y, Wang Q, Yaspan BL, Yu TW, Yurkiewicz IR, Beaudet AL, Cantor RM,

Curland M, Grice DE, Günel M, Lifton RP, Mane SM, Martin DM, Shaw CA, Sheldon M, Tischfield JA, Walsh CA, Morrow EM, Ledbetter DH, Fombonne E, Lord C, Martin CL, Brooks AI, Sutcliffe JS, Cook EH Jr, Geschwind D, Roeder K, Devlin B, State MW. Multiple recurrent de novo CNVs, including duplications of the 7q11.23 Williams syndrome region, are strongly associated with autism. *Neuron*. 2011 Jun 9;70(5):863- 85.

Schieve LA, Rice C, Devine O, Maenner MJ, Lee LC, Fitzgerald R, Wingate MS, Schendel D, Pettygrove S, van Naarde Braun K, Durkin M. Have secular changes in perinatal risk factors contributed to the recent autism prevalence increase? Development and application of a mathematical assessment model. *Ann. Epidemiol.* 2011 Dec;21(12):930-45.

Schmidt RJ, Hansen RL, Hartiala J, Allayee H, Schmidt LC, Tancredi DJ, Tassone F, Hertz-Picciotto I. Prenatal vitamins, one-carbon metabolism gene variants, and risk for autism. *Epidemiology*. 2011 Jul;22(4):476-85.

Shandley K, Austin DW. Ancestry of pink disease (infantile acrodynia) identified as a risk factor for autism spectrum disorders. *J. Toxicol. Environ. Health A*. 2011 Sep 15;74(18):1185-94.

Stamova B, Green PG, Tian Y, Hertz-Picciotto I, Pessah IN, Hansen R, Yang X, Teng J, Gregg JP, Ashwood P, Van de Water J, Sharp FR. Correlations between gene expression and mercury levels in blood of boys with and without autism. *Neurotox. Res.* 2011 Jan:19(1):31-48.

Volk HE, Hertz-Picciotto I, Delwiche L, Lurmann F, McConnell R. Residential proximity to freeways and autism in the CHARGE study. *Environ. Health Perspect.* 2011 Jun;119(6):873-7.

Question 4: Which Treatments and Interventions Will Help?

Blair K-S C, Lee I-S, Cho S-J, Dunlap G. Positive behavior support through family-school collaboration for young children with autism. *Topics in Early Childhood Special Education.* 2011 May;30(1):22-36.

Hopkins IM, Gower MW, Perez TA, Smith DS, Amthor FR, Wimsatt FC, Biasini FJ. Avatar assistant: improving social skills in students with an ASD through a computer-based intervention. *J. Aut. Dev. Disord.* 2011 Nov;41(11):1543-55.

Kasari C, Locke J, Gulsrud A, Rotheram-Fuller, E. Social networks and friendships at school: comparing children with and without ASD. *J. Autism Dev. Disord.* 2011 May;41(5):533-44.

Kim JE, O'Sullivan ML, Sanchez CA, Hwang M, Israel MA, Brennand K, Deerinck TJ, Goldstein LS, Gage FH, Ellisman MH, Ghosh A. Investigating synapse formation and function using human pluripotent stem cell-derived neurons. *Proc. Natl. Acad. Sci. USA.* 2011 Feb. 15;108(7):3005-10.

Krishnaswami S, McPheeters ML, Veenstra-Vanderweele J. A systematic review of secretin for children with autism spectrum disorders. *Pediatrics.* 2011 May;127(5):e1322-5.

Landa RJ, Holman KC, O'Neill AH, Stuart EA. Intervention targeting development of socially synchronous engagement in toddlers with autism spectrum disorder: a randomized controlled trial. *J. Child Psychol. Psychiatry.* 2011 Jan;52(1):13-21.

McPheeters ML, Warren Z, Sathe N, Bruzek JL, Krishnaswami S, Jerome RN, Veenstra-Vanderweele J. A systematic review of medical treatments for children with autism spectrum disorders. *Pediatrics.* 2011 May;127(5):e1312-21.

Paşca SP, Portmann T, Voineagu I, Yazawa M, Shcheglovitov A, Paşca AM, Cord B, Palmer TD, Chikahisa S, Nishino S, Bernstein JA, Hallmayer J, Geschwind DH, Dolmetsch RE. Using iPSC-derived neurons to uncover cellular phenotypes associated with Timothy syndrome. *Nat. Med.* 2011 Nov 27;17(12):1657-62.

Strain PS, Bovey EH. Randomized, controlled trial of the LEAP model of early intervention for young children with autism spectrum disorders. *Topics in Early Childhood Special Education.* 2011 Nov;31(3):133-154.

Strain, P, Wilson, K, Dunlap, G. Prevent-Teach-Reinforce: addressing problem behaviors of students with autism in general education classrooms. *Behavioral Disorders*. 2011 May;36(3):160–171.

Question 5: Where Can I Turn for Services?

Mandell D, Dingfelder H. Bridging the research-to-practice gap in autism intervention: an application of diffusion of innovation theory. *J. Autism Dev. Disord.* 2011 May;41:597-609.

Pickett J, Xiu E, Tuchman R, Dawson G, Lajonchere C. Mortality in individuals with autism, with and without epilepsy. *J. Child Neurol.* 2011 Aug;26(8):932-9.

Shattuck PT, Wagner M, Narendorf S, Sterzing P, Hensley M. Post-high school service use among young adults with an autism spectrum disorder. *Arch. Pediatr. Adolesc. Med.* 2011 Feb;165(2):141-6.

Question 6: What Does the Future Hold, Particularly for Adults?

Brugha TS, McManus S, Bankart J, Scott F, Purdon S, Smith J, Bettington P, Jenkins R, Meltzer, H. Epidemiology of autism spectrum disorders in adults in the community in England. *Arch. Gen. Psychiatry.* 2011 May;68(5):459-65.

Cimera R, Burgess S. Do adults with autism benefit monetarily from working in their communities? *J. Vocat. Rehabil.* 2011;34(3):173-80.

Nonnemacher SL, Bambara LM. "I'm supposed to be in charge": self-advocates' perspectives on their self-determination support needs. *Intellect Dev .Disabil.* 2011 Oct;49(5):327-40.

Piven J, Rabins P; Autism-in-Older Adults Working Group. Autism spectrum disorders in older adults: Toward defining a research agenda. *J. Am. Geriatr. Soc.* 2011 Nov;59(11):2151-55.

Stock SE, Davies DK, Wehmeyer ML, Lachapelle Y. Emerging new practices in technology to support independent community access for people with intellectual and cognitive disabilities. *NeuroRehabilitation.* 2011;28(3):261-9.

Question 7: What Other Infrastructure and Surveillance Needs Must Be Met?

Boyle CA, Boulet S, Schieve LA, Cohen RA, Blumberg SJ, Yeargin-Allsopp M, Visser S, Kogan MD. Trends in the prevalence of developmental disabilities in US children 1997-2008. *Pediatrics.* 2011 Jun;127(6):1034-42.

Kim YS, Leventhal BL, Koh YJ, Fombonne E, Laska E, Lim EC, Cheon KA, Kim SJ, Kim YK, Lee H, Song DH, Grinker RR. Prevalence of autism spectrum disorders in a total population sample. *Am. J. Psychiatry.* 2011 Sep;168(9):904-12.

INDEX

A

B

C

D

E

I

J

K

L

M

N

O

P

T